1977

Royal couple's first child Victoria Ingrid Alice Dési-rée born, Sweden's Crown Princess and Duchess of Västergötland.

1979

Carl Philip Edmund Bertil born, Prince of Sweden and Duke of Värmland.

1980

Parliament amends the Act of Succession of 1810 to allow women to ascend the throne in Sweden. King's eldest child now heir to the throne.

1981

Royal Family move out of the Royal Palace in Stockholm to take up residence at Drottningholm Palace.

1982

Madeleine Thérèse Amelie Josephine born, Princess of Sweden and Duchess of Hälsingland and Gästrikland.

1993

King celebrates the 20th anniversary of his reign. His wife Queen Silvia celebrates her 50th birthday.

1994

The Swedish authorities reduce the age at which the heir may inherit the throne from 25 to 18 in line with the age of majority for other Swedes.

1995

King's eldest child Crown Princess Victoria is 18 and takes on representative duties as well as standing in for her father the king in his absence.

1996

King Carl XVI Gustaf is 50. He has been king for 23 years.

FOR SWEDEN
CARL XVI GUSTAF
IN KEEPING WITH THE TIMES

for Sweden

CARL XVI GUSTAF
IN KEEPING
WITH THE TIMES

Lena Rainer

28766

Pictures: **Sydsvenskan's Archives, Bernadotte Library, Pressens Bild, Pica Pressfoto, IBL and Bild & Media Productions**
Cover Pictures: **JanErik Henriksson 1992 and Björn Larsson Ask 1995**

Text: **LENA RAINER**
Picture Editor: **PER LINDSTRÖM**
Layout: **INGEBORG ANDERSSON**
Illustrator: **PETTER LÖNEGÅRD**
Translation: **PETER ETHERDEN, Rye, England**
Print **Trydells Tryckeri AB, Laholm 1996**
Colour Repro: **Offset–Repro, Halmstad**
Paper: **Multi Art Silk, 150 gm**
Typeface: **New Baskerville, Trajan, Futura, Snell Roundhand**

Publisher: **Sydsvenskan, S–205 05 Malmö 040–28 12 00**
Copyright: **Sydsvenskan and specified originators**
ISBN 91–972798–0–3

CONTENTS

This book is about Sweden's king, Carl XVI Gustaf, and is published by Sydsvenskan to celebrate the king's 50th birthday on 30th April 1996. The book is about the king's upbringing and what he does in his private and public life. Some forty interviews were conducted with people who are, or used to be, close to the king at different times during his life: school mates, party friends, politicians of every persuasion, hunting companions, girlfriends, people in business, courtiers, local councillors, provincial governors, republicans and royalists. And then some. To all of them and to everybody else who has contributed to the book, from all of us at Sydsvenskan, a very warm thank you.

King Carl Gustaf XVI's 30th April birthday celebrations in the palace yard have become a popular and much loved tradition over the years. The king enjoys these occasions with their opportunities for spontaneity and laughter. And who wouldn't want to celebrate their birthday like this?
PHOTO: JANERIK HENRIKSSON 1992

A TALE OF TWO REHEARSALS.

Sweden is in mourning. Three days ago the old king Gustav VI Adolf died in Helsingborg at the age of 90. Tomorrow, 19 September 1973, Sweden's new king, Carl Gustaf will take his royal oath and present his king's name and motto to the government, parliament and the Swedish people.

This will take place in the Council Chamber and in the Great Hall at the Palace in the presence of the court, the government, the heads of the country's civil and military authorities, the knights of the Swedish Order of Seraphims, the attorney general and many others. But just now, the day before, preparations are in full swing in The Great Hall.

Silver crowns are polished. The throne's canopy is dusted. The stone floor is scrubbed.

In the midst of all this activity, the king is in rehearsal at the throne. His youngest sister Princess Christina, Prince Bertil, First Marshal of the Court Tom Wachtmeister and an aide Einar Lyth have volunteered their services.

During his time as Crown Prince, the King was not exactly renowned for the strength of his voice or the clarity of his diction. Even at its best the king's rather timid murmurs call for the help of a microphone.

So it comes as something of a shock to the assembled company standing around the stone floor in their mourning clothes, to discover that the venerable Great Hall built in 1775 has no loudspeaker system.

Here the king has to speak loudly and clearly to be heard during the ceremony the next day. Loudspeakers have never been used before, so loudspeakers will not be used tomorrow. Thus spoke the guardians of tradition. Instead, and quickly, the king must learn to speak louder!

The young king takes his place before the silver throne designed by Magnus Gabriel De la Gardie and presented to Queen Kristina for her coronation in Stockholm's Great Church in 1650.

Under the large blue canopy, added 100 years later for the coronation of Adolf Frederik in 1751, the king begins to flex his vocal chords.

The others trot down to the farthest corner of the hall to listen.

"We Carl Gustaf, King of Sweden, do hereby acclaim..." the king begins.

It sounds like an gnat in a desert. Nobody hears a word.

– Louder, shout the producers far down the hall.

It was a historic occasion when the new king addressed the Swedish Parliament in September 1973. A breakthrough for Carl Gustaf, many thought. Pictures of the disco-loving Crown Prince began to fade away, replaced by images of an ambitious and dutiful head of state.
PHOTO: JAN COLLSIÖÖ 1973

Beneath the throne's canopy the king tries again. His voice is drowned in the rococo marble; his words lost. Tomorrow these words will be more sonorous and stately as befits a speech from the throne composed under the guidance of poets like Bo Setterlind.

– Try harder! Louder! shout Wachtmeister and Lyth, as the king comes close to bursting:

"We Carl Gustaf, King of Sweden, do hereby acclaim..." yells the king.

Prince Bertil is still not satisfied:

– Imitate my gin and tonic bass voice; that should work better, roars Uncle Nappe who is in charge of the rehearsal.

Everyone laughs and begins to relax again.

Afterwards the king promises to practise that evening. So in his private palace apartment, with Christina as a strict but loyal coach, the king puts in some hard training for his debut the next day.

With the doors to the apartment's ten rooms wide open and with Christina and Carl Gustaf as far apart as possible, the palace echoes long into the night with the sound of the king's address from the throne.

Do you remember how it went the next day?

It was something of a breakthrough for Carl XVI Gustaf.

Bo Setterlind is sitting at home in front of the television in Strängnäs keeping his fingers crossed. But seeing how impressive the ceremony is and how well the king is coping, he immediately packs his wife and children into the car and drives the thirty miles to Stockholm to be among the crowds outside the palace cheering the king in the evening.

And in the media, reviewers talk of a success.

Sydsvenskan writes in its editorial:

"During the ceremony in the Great Hall Carl XVI Gustaf made a valuable contribution in the role he has inherited from Gustav VI Adolf."

The palace breathes again. At least on this occasion.

Another rehearsal – under happier circumstances – in the same venerable hall. It is Summer 1995, the day before Crown Princess Victoria comes of age. In the Great Hall the final preparations are under way for a royal occasion that is being broadcast live on TV the next day.

Everyone is in a flutter, nervous, anxious to ensure that the occasion goes as well as it possibly can. There is no protocol for the ceremony. No Swedish Bernadotte Crown Princess has come of age before. So there is a mood of improvisation in the air. Music, flowers, procession, pages?

Father, the king, is in place. So are the Marshal of the Realm, First Marshal of the Court and other palace aides.

And then Victoria arrives, the centre of attention, skipping between the marble statues.

Denim miniskirt, brown T-shirt, ponytail. Trainers.

Sweden's Crown Princess is in fine spirits. Tomorrow's seriousness with its classic long dress, severe hairstyle and Seraphim Order decorations are far away in the future.

Here there is an ordinary lively seventeen and a half year old who cannot resist poking fun at the serious court dignitaries in the Great Hall and at her ever more stressed father.

Victoria immediately spies the magnificent old silver drums hidden away under the throne. She knows it is the apple of her father's eye, ordered by him especially for the next day's ceremony.

– Who is to be christened? Who put that old font there?

The Crown Princess giggles and sets everybody else off. Not even the king manages to keep a straight face.

And so to rehearsals. The king has gone to great pains to think through the various details. Who will be in the procession? How are they to enter and exit? How should room be made for the general public? Indeed it is the king's own idea to allow the public into the inner courtyard to congratulate Victoria after the official ceremony, before she receives the cheers of the crowds along Lejonbacken and on Norrbro.

Victoria and the silver throne. – Your Majesty. Dear Father... In front of The Kingdom of Sweden's grandest possession, the silver throne, the 18-year old Crown Princess Victoria makes her first official speech to King Carl Gustaf. The throne was a gift for Queen Kristina's coronation in 1650 from Magnus De la Gardie.
PHOTO: TOBIAS RÖSTLUND 1995

But the king is not keen to have too many flowers inside the Great Hall – this is not a school graduation ceremony. In the end the king is persuaded that it would look nice with flowers in front of the lectern and under the throne canopy:

– OK, just a few bunches then.

How should the king and Victoria move, stand and sit at different times? When the king speaks Victoria stands and listens, the king decides.

When the Marshal of the Realm strikes his grand staff on the floor it is Victoria's turn to speak. With a powerful and clear voice, technically trained at Dramaten by the actress Margaretha Krook, she will deliver the words "Your Majesty, Dear Father..." and the king will sit down.

– You mean father sits down but I have to stand up?

Father should stand, while I speak insists the insubordinate teenager.

Court dignitaries shuffle uncomfortably and look away.

This time the king does not give in. His protesting daughter is ordered to do what her father tells her.

– No, you stand and I sit. There's a right and a wrong way to do things.

They move on to the next matter. Once it gets particularly tense with the king wanting one thing, the court dignitaries another and Victoria something else. Stalemate. What to do?

– I know, exclaims Victoria, a twinkle in her eye as she looks at the king.

– We don't bother with my 18th birthday. We abandon the idea and celebrate my 19th birthday next year instead. Then there's no problem!

Everybody laughs. Afterwards it all sorts itself out anyway.

And Victoria's Coming of Age is a success, a moving celebration that shed many a tear.

Most moved of all was the master of ceremony himself.

Her father, the king.

Proud, happy and relieved. A happy family trio relaxes after Victoria's successful debut as Crown Princess of Sweden. Once she has reached the age of 18, the Crown Princess can be called upon at any time to represent her country whenever her father is otherwise engaged.
PHOTO: TOBIAS RÖSTLUND 1995

Students gather around a beer crate outside the palace while waiting to form a guard of honour at the coming of age of Crown Princess Victoria.
PHOTO: JONAS LEMBERG 1995

THE KING AND I.

Like most people in their forties I was - raised on a 50s and 60s diet of cute and rather seductive royal reporting of happy hours at Haga with the little prince.

These idyllic reports about the king's children then gave way to the republican issue, the rise of the left and pictures of the energetic disco-prince having a good time at Alexandra's. Many thought there was no way he would ever be suitable as a king and a valued ambassador for Sweden, while I took little interest in the matter and was quite indifferent to the king as a person.

During my years as a journalist with Expressen and Sydsvenskan I covered several occasions where the crown prince/the king was involved: cabinet meetings where a new minister of state swore his oath of allegiance, the official state opening of parliament, Carl Gustaf's coronation in the Great Hall, the Nobel Prize ceremonies and so on.

My lack of interest turned into a sort of sympathy. This shy, easily embarrassed novice of a king played his part as well as could be expected within the constraints of a stuffy ceremonial tradition and a liturgy which he could do little to influence. Poor thing, born to this.

In 1993 Sydsvenskan's editor-in-chief, Jan Wifstrand asked me to interview the king.

Sure, why not? Ask anything you like, Jan suggested. Write to Elisabeth Tarras-Wahlberg at the king's private office and ask.

The king had grown up without a father and was now the father of teenage children. How did he get on with his role as father without a father figure of his own? How had the loss of his father affected him as a person and as a father? Did he lack a sense of fatherhood?

I was living with a similar situation so it was quite natural for me to choose the absence of a father, the role of a father and the worries of parenting as the themes of my questions for the king.

And he said yes!

So that was how I came to meet the king on two separate occasions and how I came to have my preconceptions about him torn to shreds. On the first occasion I accompanied him on a state visit, and on the other occasion I interviewed the king himself.

A long time ahead of the scheduled interview I travelled with the royal couple on a state visit to Germany in order to study the king at closer quarters during a few particularly busy days in his state visit.

Experienced royal reporter colleagues were happy to assure me that on this trip the king would be morose and obstinate. Queen

Goodness, what a lot of pictures there are in the archives! The book's author Lena Rainer finds one picture she remembers from her childhood as incredibly dramatic.
PHOTO: PER LINDSTRÖM 1995

Silvia is half-German and so she is admired in Germany even more than in Sweden, if that is possible. Germans look upon Queen Silvia as their queen, "unsere Königin", and worship her whenever she sets foot on her native soil.

The king finds this adoration difficult to take, my colleagues explained. He is used to being the centre of attention and dislikes being upstaged in "royalness" and admiration, even if the rival happens to be his wife.

But these colleagues were completely wrong. They were correct about Queen Silvia. Everywhere they went, in Bonn, Lützen, Wittenberg, Berlin and Stralsund, happy Germans greeted them in droves, deluging the queen with flowers, cheering and waving and taking pictures.

But the king was not at all surly and sulky. In fact he held back diplomatically and allowed the enormous popularity of the queen full rein as she continued her triumphal march through Germany to the adoration of the German people. The king let her go a step ahead of him while standing to one side smiling.

Tactful, considerate and really nice, were my thoughts. Any idea that he would be sulky must have been meant as a joke. In my book he had earned himself one large brownie point.

My next meeting with the king took place when I interviewed him in his palace apartment some weeks later. I was well prepared, having planned millions of questions.

The interview took barely an hour but it was long enough for my image of a reserved, timid and rather tongue–tied monarch to change completely.

The king was cheerful, unexpectedly helpful and would evade my questions with a friendly little laugh whenever he felt they went too far. He was serious and thoughtful when it came to the difficult questions about his father's early death and what it had meant for him. And as a father he was deeply concerned about his teenage children's exposure to drugs.

When I countered that there was not much risk of drug dealers getting past governesses, limousine chauffeurs and palace aides to slip the king's children some drugs, he refused to hear a word of it.

Drugs were to be found in all classes of society, he said, and his children were no more protected from them than anybody else. Drugs were everywhere and it was this that made it a particularly nasty problem.

We spoke of the king's own childhood, about bringing up children, the daily routines of a king, the future, publicity, homework and his personal security. Some weeks later the interview was published as a double page feature article in Sydsvenskan.

The monarch I met was friendly and open, quick to laugh, ready to make amusing asides, entreating me on occasions, seeking my understanding. His vocabulary might be a little limited at times, but he chose his words with care and made sure he said what he meant.

The king was not shy, morose and inarticulate as I had expected and had prepared myself for. Indeed at the risk of being labelled a snob or a social climber I admit that although I did not fall for him, I certainly found myself warming towards his royal highness as a person.

Dull, stiff, formal, boring to some. Warm, considerate, spontaneous, fun to others. Dr Jekyll and Mr Hyde? Who was he actually, our king?

My curiosity was aroused. When my editor Jan Wifstrand later asked me to write a book about the king for his 50th birthday I therefore said yes. I wanted to find out just who it was hiding behind the mask.

His great grandfather Gustav V is dead and Carl Gustaf is Crown Prince of Sweden at the age of four. Solemn and upset he attends the funeral of the old king in the company of the new queen Louise and his mother Sibylla who are dressed in the beautiful traditional court mourning gowns. *BM BILD 1950*

20

growing up

– ES IST EIN ...
BOY ...GEBOREN.

Shortly after 10.20 on April 30th in the year 1946 the kingdom of Sweden sighed with relief.

Princess Sibylla had given birth to her fifth child, a bonny male heir, who was happily oblivious of the relief sweeping the country as he slept peacefully in Karl XI's old cradle at Haga Palace outside Stockholm.

Peeping over the edge of the antique cradle were his four fair-haired Haga sisters, in wide-eyed admiration of their wrinkly little brother, but well aware of how remarkable he already was. His mother Sibylla was probably exhausted, but his father Gustav Adolf rang round to all the relatives to tell them the good news.

At the royal palace in Stockholm King Gustav V – 88 years old and the young boy's great grandfather – received the happy announcement while busy with his embroidery, while grandfather Crown Prince Gustav Adolf probably allowed himself a small glass of celebratory sherry with his wife Crown Princess Louise.

EXTRABLAD
SYDSVENSKA DAGBLADET
SNÄLLPOSTEN

Tisdagen den   30 april 1946

ARVPRINS
av Sverige

STOCKHOLM den 30. (TT)

Prinsessan Sibylla nedkom tisdag förmiddag med en son. Den lyckliga tilldragelsen ägde rum på Haga, och den nyfödde prinsen hälsades med salut, 84 skott i två omgångar med 42 skott i varje, från salutbatterierna vid Stockholms, Karlskrona och Göteborgs örlogsstationer och i Stockholms och Blekinge kustartilleriförsvar samt från salutpliktiga örlogsfartyg.

Everybody rejoiced when Sweden finally had a male heir. Sydsvenskan published their first and only special supplement.

Father Gustav Adolf rang his old Austro-Hungarian friend Prince Alexander Erba Odescalchi, a refugee in Sweden in the war, to inform him of the new addition to the family: the longed-for son. In his excitement the proud father forgot the German for boy,'Junge' and took the Swedish word 'pojke' instead:

– Es its ein...pojke... geboren, he declared joyfully.

– I'll never forget it, recounted Prince Alexander, now 83 years old.

All over Sweden flags were run up flagpoles, no doubt with considerable relief, as the May Day festivities got under way. In Skeppsholmen Church, Te Deums were sung and over the Stockholm Canal cannons boomed out their traditional salute.

Normally 21 shots are fired for the birth of a royal child with twice as many, 42 shots, for a first child or an heir to the throne. On this occasion 84 shots were fired into the April mist over Stockholm's still waters! Everyone was so overjoyed at the birth of a

A historic picture of four generations of Bernadottes. Father Gustav Adolf and Grandfather Crown Prince Gustav Adolf admire the newly christened Carl Gustaf lying in Great Grandfather Gustav V's lap. Carl Gustaf is already Duke of Jämtland and a member of the Knight Order of Seraphims. The Order's light blue sash is draped across him. *BERNADOTTEBIBLIOTEKET 1946*

The big sisters' darling Carl Gustaf is of course the centre of attraction in the first Christmas portrait from Haga Palace. From left to right, Désirée age 7, Margaretha 11, Birgitta 9 and Christina 3.

PHOTO: SIV NEUTERBOOM 1946

The Knight Order of Seraphims takes its name from the highest class of angel. The order was founded in 1748 and in 1974 the government decided that membership should no longer be open to ordinary Swedish citizens. The late Marcus Wallenberg and Sten Rudholm were the last commoners to receive the title. Royal knights of the order are the King, Queen Silvia, Prince Bertil, Princess Lilian, the King's four sisters Margaretha, Birgitta, Désirée and Christina, and the widowed Queen Ingrid. Foreign royalty and heads of state are still awarded the Swedish Order of Seraphims, England's Queen Elizabeth and Iceland's President Vigdís Finnbogadóttir being among them. IHS stands for Iesus Hominum Salvator – Jesus Saviour of Mankind.

PHOTO: PER LINDSTRÖM 1996

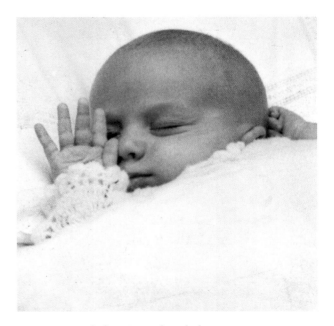

A very young little prince already busy practising his royal wave.
H ILLUSTRATIONSBYRÅ 1946

The two-year old little prince Carl Gustaf, honorary member of the Field Cavalry Club being saluted by his inferior rank, Colonel Wrede. *PHOTO: H NYRÉN 1948*

Only Queen Silvia and the king's relations may call the king Carl Gustaf. Everyone else must address the king as Your Majesty or by the more familiar King

Swedish Flag Day, June the 6th, together with mother Sibylla and great grandfather Gustav V
PHOTO: BO DAHLIN 1949

male heir that special permission was given for the twice double royal salute. A week later the infant child was christened Carl Gustaf Folke Hubertus in the palace chapel by Archbishop Erling Eidem. Carl and Gustaf were proud ancient royal names, and so were no surprise. Gustaf was in honour of great grandfather Gustav V, grandfather Gustav Adolf and his father Gustav Adolf. And Carl was in honour of his mother's German father Karl Eduard of Sachsen-Coburg Gotha.

The little prince took the name Folke after Folke Bernadotte, murdered by the Stern terrorist gang two years later. The unexpected Hubertus was in memory of Sibylla's cherished brother killed in the war. So Carl Gustaf Folke Hubertus it was. Splendid names, yet while he was a child, the Swedish people would always refer to him as 'Lillprinsen' – The Little Prince.
It was 1946 and the honours started pouring in thick and fast. He was Duke of Jämtland and a member of the Knight Order

This picture must melt the hearts of the most hardened republicans, for cuter than this is hard to imagine. Carl Gustaf trying on his smart uniform, model y.

PHOTO: EINAR JAGERWALL

of Seraphims before he was through his first packet of nappies and an Honorary Wolf Cub before he had time to raise his eyebrows – his father was of course President of the Swedish Scout Council.

All was sweetness and light for the large family at Haga Palace. The eldest sister Margaretha was 11, Birgitta 9, Désirée 7 and Christina 3.

But the family bliss lasted only nine months. Just long enough to take the happy family photograph with Carl Gustaf in his mother Sibylla's arms, the shy but curious elder sisters and his father Gustav Adolf, erect and proud, a protective paternal eye cast over his happy brood.

And there was just enough time to take the classic picture of three generations of solemn royal gentlemen in ceremonial dress with their shining pointed stars, with the latest addition of a fourth, a little bundle of soft fluffy embroidery, in their midst. Just time for the pictures before life at Haga changed for ever. In fact it changed for all of us in the Kingdom of Sweden. A complete generation of royal heirs was wiped out and there was a gap in the succession.

On a grey cold January day in 1947 the dramatic news came over the radio that the heir to the Swedish throne Gustav Adolf had been killed in a plane crash at Kastrup Airport. He had been hunting in Holland and had stopped over in Copenhagen. On his way home to Stockholm, the plane took off normally but then broke up 30 seconds later and crashed to the ground. Everybody on board, 22 people in all, died instantly in the inferno.

The air crash was Scandinavia's "biggest and most appalling", declared Sydsvenskan on its front page the next day. What Gustav Adolf's untimely death must have meant for Sibylla – at 39 a widow locked away in a golden royal cage – and her five children we can only speculate.

For Prince Bertil, apart from the personal loss, the death of his elder brother Gustav Adolf meant a dramatic incursion in his own adult life. He loyally did his duty for almost 40 years, securing the succession, before finally putting his own life first and marrying Lilian Craig in 1976 at the age of 64.

The little prince Carl Gustaf made his official debut on 16 June 1948. His Great Grandfather King Gustav V celebrated his 90th birthday and was honoured by his loyal subjects with a procession through Stockholm. The 2-year old little prince went along on his

mother Sibylla's knee. The Haga family's long-serving child nurse, nanny and mummy–substitute, Nenne Björnberg writes in her memoires of the lively discussions that took place beforehand on the correct placing of the potty in the royal landau "for all eventualities".

– But it really wasn't needed, she protested rather indignantly.

Out at Haga the little prince is into everything and anything. He is busy digging pits according to one newspaper, building castles (and falling off one to be rushed to a doctor for stitches), playing with cars and doing everything a normal active child should do at that age.

When the little prince is two years old the press photographers descend on Haga to record the event, making this perhaps the king's first encounter with the media.

– Silly people, the little prince remarks

29

Dressed up in his best clothes for an official occasion. Little Carl Gustaf elegantly dressed with matching coat and leggings worn over his shoes. Many of his clothes were actually made up or were altered by the palace seamstress Miss Jansson who served the Bernadotte family for many years. Miss Jansson still made Carl Gustaf's pyjamas after he was king.
PHOTO: TORE EKHOLM 1949

about the photographers.

On his third birthday he receives a pedal car from Uncle Nappe, Prince Bertil, the motor car prince. Big Success! The little prince is also shown shovelling broken ice into a wheelbarrow from a frozen lake. The newspapers shows the picture of this charming little snowman, but the reaction from a worried public is instantaneous:

– Fancy letting him play on the ice? Don't they realise he is heir to the throne?

The public also worries that he is 'a little bow-legged'. He is a happy and playful child, though already awfully shy. Hearing old ladies and their "Ah, isn't he sweet!" – and he hears this a lot – is enough to make him upset and run away.

His big sister Christina, Titti, is his best friend and his closest playmate. They bake gingerbread together and ride ponies, lots of ponies over the years: Rosita, Don Basilo and Pony Don. He has his share of rows with his sisters of course. Once the little prince chased Titti trying to soak her with a glass of water.

– Dustaf is a man, Dustaf does dare, shouts the little prince, already aware of his role as a man.

This picture caused a minor storm in the media. – Fancy letting him play on the ice by himself? Our heir to the thone! The public were shocked by this dangerous springtime game, not realising that the ice was at the edge of a lake and there were sisters and the family's life-long child nurse Nenne Björnberg watching him. *AB TEXT & BILDER 1949*

Old Man and Young Child. The 90-year old King Gustav V and his two-year old great grandson Carl Gustaf enjoying a game of croquet in the summer of 1948. The picture prompts thoughts of the old year giving way to a new year full of promise.
PHOTO: E BENGTSSON 1948

Christina, Titti, is the youngest of all Carl Gustaf's sisters and from the start his closest friend and playmate. Here the young gentleman is pouring out some squash for Titti at the traditional mid-December royal photo session.
SKÅNEREPORTAGE 1948

There seems to be some dispute about the way Carl Gustaf should drive his first and much loved pedal car. Not surprisingly it was Prince Bertil, the car enthusiast Uncle Nappe, who gave the car to the little prince as a present on his third birthday.
SVENSKT PRESSFOTO 1949

His big sisters retaliate, once hiding their baby brother in a broom cupboard. His nurse and his mother are beside themselves with anxiety and search every room in the palace fearing the worst may have happened to their, and all of Sweden's, little prince, but he eventually turns up safe and well. Every parent knows how that feels.

In 1950 Haga Palace has to be renovated so the family leave their green park and their familiar playgrounds and move temporarily into Queen Victoria's empty ten-room apartment in the Royal Palace in Stockholm. The family are due to return to Haga a year later. But they enjoy themselves so much in town that they eventually decide to stay.

Hanging out of the palace windows are now five wide-eyed "country kids" taking in all the new attractions of a big city: buses, trams, excavators, steam boats and the changing of the guards – a sensation!

Meanwhile the endless palace corridors offer the little prince the ideal racing circuit for his beloved pedal car while the garden with its

Before the days of jeans – his first proper pair of long trousers. Carl Gustaf trying out his nicely fitting breeches on the lawn at Tullgarn before the start of his third birthday party.
PHOTO: BERTIL FORSÉN 1949

All the anxiety at his great grandfather's funeral gets to be too much for the little four year old crown prince. As his grandfather Gustav Adolf VI goes to leave the palace to greet the well-wishers on Lejonbacken, Carl Gustaf is frightened by the camera flashbulbs. He bursts out crying and rushes for the comfort of his grandfather's arms. In the background is Prince Wilhelm, son of the dead King Gustav V. *PHOTO: ILGARS LINDE 1950*

The little prince spent the whole of his childhood surrounded by women: his mother Sibylla, his four sisters and his nurse Nenne Björnberg who lived on at the palace in Stockholm until her death in 1994.
BERNADOTTEBIBLIOTEKET 1950

specially installed sand box is perfect.

Moreover his mother Sibylla and his nanny Nenne are delighted to discover that colds and ear infections are ills of the past caused it seems by the dampness of Haga.

On 11 October 1950 their landlord, King Gustav V, arrives to "inspect" his new tenants at the Royal Palace. Clean-up time! He is their great grandfather, but the children call him "Grandfather King". All the little prince knows is that his waxed moustache tickles.

Just over two weeks later, on 29 October, Grandfather King dies, 92 years old. Incredibly he had been Sweden's head of state for 43 years, 1907–1950, and reigned during two world wars.

The Haga family are alone in the 650-room royal palace. At the age of four, the heir to the Swedish throne Carl Gustaf is now Crown Prince.

...I Refuse
To Be King.

W hen Gustav V was buried on November 9th 1950 the Crown Prince watched the procession from one of the palace's 900 windows. Some journalists noticed this and cabled the news around the world. The alarm went up at once. The little prince could fall out! The Palace responded with safety latches on palace windows, although not on all 900 of them.

When the prince was six he started nursery school at the palace, supervised by Brita Schlyter and attended by a few children from "better families", Rutger Uggla, Erland Broman, Christoffer Murray, Carl Johan Smith, Henrik Kugelberg and Carl Gustaf Ekman. Their teacher explained to the other boys that the little prince was no different to anybody else except that he must be addressed as "Crown Prince" and not with the familiar "du" normally used by Swedish children among themselves.

The prince also attended a craft school on Linnégatan. He loved this because he was allowed to make and do things properly. The little prince's father and his three eldest sisters had begun their schooling at the palace. So there were many raised eyebrows when the Palace announced that the little prince would attend a 'normal' school, the private Anna Broms

On Swedish Flag Day the five year old Carl Gustaf rides in an open carriage with King Gustav Adolf and his mother Sibylla in a procession through the streets of Stockholm. *SVENSKT PRESSFOTO 1951*

Christmas is on the way and his mother Sibylla helps seal the presents. *SYDSVENSKAN 1950*

36

The little prince Carl Gustaf, his nanny Ingrid Björnberg and Princess Christina arrive back at Stockholm's Central Railway Station after a wonderful time at Solliden.
Ingrid Nenne Björnberg was taken on as a child nurse at Haga Palace in 1938 for two years. But she was to stay almost fifty years with the royal family. Her dreams of further education and a family of her own were sacrificed to provide care and security for the five children after the loss of their father.
SANDELS ILLUSTRATIONSBYRÅ 1951

school on Sturegatan. The decision was the result of much discussion, with Princess Sibylla emerging victorious. In her opinion a palace school would be much too small and the crown prince would benefit from being part of a larger school class.

On his first day at school, 8 September 1952, he was photographed at his desk surrounded by his classmates, some of them friends who had followed him from nursery school and some still his friends today: Carl Johan Smith, Magnus Wickman, Carl Kleman, Hans Jörgen Zetterström (nicknamed 'Anckarström' after getting into a fight with the crown prince!), Henrik Kugelberg, Hans von der Groeben, Erland Broman and others.

Each day Nenne took the prince to Sturegatan and back again. They walked together through the centre of Stockholm, from Sturegatan, over Norrmalmstorg, through Kungsträdgården and home to the palace. There was no thought of bodyguards in those idyllic times. The prince did not find it embarassing to be fetched every day nor did it worry him to hold his nanny's hand in front of his classmates. In fact if he tried really hard he could persuade Nenne to buy him a hot dog in Norrmalmstorg on the way home. Here they would wander around chatting about the goings-on of the day. According to Nenne the walk home took absolutely ages because the prince insisted on inspecting every hole (the underground train system was under construction in Stockholm during the 1950s) and stopping to watch the workmen and their mechanical diggers.

He was inquisitive and never stopped asking questions. On one occasion one of the workmen turned to him and said: – Shut up, you little brat!

– I am quite certain he doesn't recognise me, said the little boy, who was already used to people doing so.

What he liked most was to lose himself in the crowd, not liking the attention and the way he was watched all the time. He hated being fussed over although he appreciated friendliness. And he thought it a shame he could not earn a few pence delivering milk like other children.

Once Christina came running in crying her eyes out and sobbing: "He hit me, he hit me, and I didn't do anything!" Upon investigation the crown prince turned out to have a somewhat different explanation:

– Titti says I'll be a king when I grow up and I won't because I'm going to be a worker.
– But that's no reason to hit someone?
– Well, I refuse to be king!

The Broms School performed short plays at the end of each year. Carl Gustaf appeared in 1957 as a much celebrated Birger Jarl. The following year, his last year at Broms, he played Karl XII, made up to look like his portrait, complete with bald head and pointed nose.

One year he had the job of 'school policeman'. Outside Swedish schools, older pupils look after the pedestrian crossings. This soon threatened to end in disaster. Word spread like wild fire and before long there were the ladies in their fur coats, rushing up for a glimpse of him. The real police were summoned to sort out the traffic jam at the prince's pedestrian crossing.

Some of the people involved in the crown prince's education at this time were Prince Bertil, Bo Ekelund (head of the Swedish Athletics Federation) and the head of the School Board at that time Nils Gustav Rosén, later University Chancellor.

Today, 40 years on, we know that at Broms the crown prince was found to be word blind, as it was called then. It seems that certain teachers refused to countenance the idea which hardly made them competent to deal with a child with learning disabilities. The legendary education consultant Alice Lundström was called in by N G Rosén to find out the facts, and yes the crown prince was dyslexic. But still the teachers were unwilling to grapple with the problem. Rosén insisted that remedial measures be taken immediately, threatening to disclaim any reponsibility for the crown prince's education if his pleas were ignored.

Prince Bertil persuaded Rosén to stay. But even when the crown prince went to Sigtuna Academy of Liberal Arts no special measures seem to have been taken.

Nonetheless Broms School suited the prince. He became bolder, tougher and even

Boy Racer. Carl Gustaf on his bike – a favourite picture from the 50s.
H STENBERGS ILLUSTRATIONSBYRÅ 1954

PHOTO: TORE EKHOLM 1951

TEXT OCH BILDER 1952

Baking gingerbread at The Royal Palace in Stockholm. No problems with concentration or interest when Prince Carl Gustaf and Princess Christina turn their hands to baking.
PHOTO: FREDDY LINDSTRÖM 1952

Big kiss for the king. Carl Gustaf's affections being passed around on Swedish Flag Day at Stockholm Stadium.

PHOTO: FREDDY LINDSTRÖM 1954

held morning service. But otherwise the prince's life went on in its own gentle way. At the palace he entertained himself with 'Svälta Räv' (Hungry Fox), and 'Svarte Petter' (Black Peter) and insisted that the best-selling 50s comics such as 'Stålmannen' (Superman) and 'Fantomen' (Phantom) should be read aloud to him.

His sisters were now old enough for young gentlemen to begin appearing in the state apartments and sometimes they would be invited to tea. Nowadays they tell how the crown prince would be on the floor with his electric train set and what fun the little prince had when "the big boys" got down on the floor and helped him with the points and signals. Other attractions for the crown prince were his visits to the Ship Museum, the Museum of Technology and the circus. The newsreels at the Spegeln cinema and Donald Duck in London and Hollywood also stood high on his list.

In Easter 1954 the whole family travelled to Storlien for their first ever skiing holiday.

– The crown prince would lose himself gazing at a beautiful view or watching the ever changing scene of the sun glinting

Now for the serious business. Prince Carl Gustaf arriving home from Solliden to begin his second year of school. Princess Sibylla abandoned the tradition of a palace schooling and allowed the little prince to go to an ordinary school, Anna Broms School on Sturegatan.
PHOTO: FREDDY LINDSTRÖM 1953

One of the first colour pictures of a serious-minded crown prince in his own room at the Royal Palace in Stockholm. *IBL 1954*

and the shadows of the clouds passing over the landscape, Nenne tells us. So perhaps it was here and during all those summers at Sibylla's Solliden that his enduring interest in nature was aroused.

As far as official business was concerned there was Swedish Flag Day at Skansen, the opening of Lill-Skansen (Little Skansen) and his debut in 1957 as an eleven-year old at the State Opening of Parliament which at the time took place in the Great Hall at the palace.

A milestone was passed in 1956 when the crown prince, an honorary wolf cub, was enrolled as a wolf cub in St. Klara Church and was given the name Mowgli. He learnt to play ice hockey, being coached at Stockholm Stadium by such Swedish 50s stars as Lasse Björn and Sven Tumba.

– The crown prince was a promising little fellow with a good eye for the game, summarised Sven Tumba in his memoires.

In May 1959 the 13-year old crown prince and his mother went on a private study visit to the Academy of Liberal Arts in Sigtuna. Could this establishment possibly be given the honour of taking the future king to his Studenten? Indeed it was. It turned out to suit the Palace and so the crown prince was enrolled there for his second year of secondary schooling, the school not having a first year class. On 31 August 1959 the crown prince left the palace and moved into student accommodation in Sigtuna. His childhood friend Carl Johan Smith went along too, to make the move easier and help him feel more at home.

43

A solemn salute to the flag on
Swedish Flag Day at the Stadium. His
Big sister Désirée is beside him and
cutting a fine figure as a princess.
TEXT&BILDER 1955

*A flag flying over the Royal Palace used to mean the king
was in residence. But not any more. Nowadays the flag is
always flying. But when the king is at home the flag
bears a large royal crest, while when the king is abroad
and the Crown Princess or Prince Bertil are deputising
for him then a smaller crest adorns the flag.*

The little prince is not even left in peace during break by the press photographers. But he ignores them enjoying himself instead with his friends Sven Hult and Carl Johan Smith.
TEXT&BILDER 1956

At present the Swedish Royal House claims six heirs to the throne, in order of succession: Crown Princess Victoria, Prince Carl Philip, Princess Madeleine, Prince Bertil, Princess Birgitta and Ingrid, Queen of Denmark.

An unusual walk to school that begins amidst the marble statues in the Royal Palace's left wing and ends at Broms School on Sturegatan. Carl Gustaf did not have bodyguards but was in no danger. Nenne Björnberg used to take him to school and back again. *TEXT&BILDER 1956*

When the little prince took his turn as an attendant at the pedestrian crossing outside Broms School it almost caused a riot. Old ladies from Östermalm vied with press photographers to get a good view and the real police had to be called in to sort out the traffic.
SYDSVENSKAN 1957

M m
O o
R r

MOR.

Mor! mor! O, mor! Orm!

King Carl Gustaf has abolished bowing and curtsying. He found the spectacle of old ladies falling to the ground in a curtsy in front of him too much to take.

At the end of Spring Term pupils at Broms School entertain parents and teachers with short plays. Guess who got to play King Karl XII?
SVENSKT PRESSFOTO 1958

48

Gymnastics was always Carl Gustaf's best subject at school and here he performs a particularly difficult vault.
TEXT&BILDER 1956

Carl Gustaf was given ice hockey lessons by such 50s stars of Swedish ice hockey as Lasse Björn (picture) and Sven Tumba. In those days there was no talk about helmets and tackle protectors.
SYDSVENSKAN 1958

Out of the sea with flippers and snorkel all ready for action on Falsterbo Beach. His interest in snorkelling would develope into a love of deep sea diving later in life.
PHOTO: HENNING STENBERG 1958

The Bernadotte Family in full regalia in the Bernadotte Gallery before the State Opening of Parliament 1958. Queen Louise, Princess Sibylla, Princess Christina and the three grown-up princesses Margaretha, Birgitta and Désirée wearing the beautiful court trains with their intricate lattice work in the sleeves and their ermine trimmings. Standing in the back row are Prince Wilhelm, King Gustav VI Adolf and Prince Bertil. The family's hope for the future, Crown Prince Carl Gustaf, is in the front.
H STENBERGS ILLUSTRATIONSBYRÅ 1958

Soon it will be your turn. King Gustav VI Adolf with his grandson Crown
Prince Carl Gustaf on the steps of Gustav Adolf's cherished Sofiero.
SYDSVENSKAN 1958

– THE OLD DEARS WITH THEIR BOX CAMERAS WERE THE WORST.

There now begins one of the happiest times in the life of the crown prince, his Sigtuna years. He is open, happy and sociable and finds it easy to make friends. Best of all, now he is away from mother, Nenne and his sisters and he has the freedom to move around by himself and experience the real world of the small town of Sigtuna at first hand.

He likes cycling into town by himself or with his friends to buy hot dogs, ice cream or sweets at Johan's corner store. He has ten kronor a week in pocket money just like all the other boys.

To begin with, in primary school, there are separate classes for girls and boys. Later on at high school classes are mixed. Friends were supposed to address the crown prince as Crown Prince, but out of earshot of the teachers, it would be "du" or Tjabo. Where Tjabo came from nobody quite knows. A pop song perhaps, or maybe it was just one of those things that happened. At high school Tjabo became Tjabbe, a name that was still sticking to him as late as 1973 when he ascended the throne. That was when the Palace rang up all his friends to advise them that the days of "du" and "Tjabbe" were over. After that even when he was with his friends he was addressed as "King" or "Your Majesty".

The crown prince did his second, third and fourth year of secondary school and then moved on into the upper school where he took the natural sciences option, switching later on to this study programme's "social" option. There was less maths, chemistry and physics here compared to the maths option, which was just as well, as the crown prince did not find the subject easy. The numbers kept skipping around. Why he did not choose the Latin option available at that time was of course because languages are even harder for someone with dyslexia, writing and reading difficulties. Later in life the king descibed his learning disability:

– I reverse vowels, which makes me slur my words sometimes when I speak.

It is no secret that he needed extra lessons during these years – an appropriate response for those with reading disabilities. But it is questionable whether the crown prince received the remedial training that dyslexia calls for.

The crown prince did well in biology, history and geography with gymnastics as his best subject. There was plenty of gym, sport

"Quite a good shot" is the text for this picture taken at a roe deer hunt on Count Otto Stenbock's estate in the Stockholm archipelago. The king is now generally regarded as an excellent shot and a discerning hunter.
STENBERGS ILLUSTRATIONSBYRÅ 1962

To start with, Carl Gustaf had to squeeze onto the "royal balcony" alongside his sisters for the State Opening of Parliament in the Great Hall and is seen here with the princesses Christina, Désirée and Margaretha. But since taking the Oath of Allegiance in 1965 he has moved down into the hall to be at the king's right hand.
REPORTAGEBILD 1966

and athletics at Sigtuna. Carl Gustaf took part in the Royal Swedish Sailing Club's sailing camps and racing, participating in the Swedish School Championships in Karlstad and receiving his first sailing boat as a present on his 18th birthday. He began to prefer downhill skiing to cross-country and outside the school's grounds the crown prince began to hunt seriously. He also took a great interest in the archeological digs taking place in and around Sigtuna, the media being quick to point out where that interest came from, his grandfather King Gustav Adolf VI being a highly respected archeologist.

Nowadays the children of the royal family are closely protected but there was not even the suggestion of a minder or bodyguard when Carl Gustaf was at Sigtuna. In the 50s and 60s danger came from quite a different quarter, the biggest "threat" to the crown prince at

Sigtuna being "old ladies with box cameras". They would come in herds to Sigtuna, often finding their way out to the academy in pursuit of their prey.

These old biddies were actually much worse than the professional photographers, who at least left the crown prince in peace between the bouts of romance rumour-mongering.

His friends used to volunteer to "cover" for the crown prince, both literally from the camera lens, and from teachers and housemasters when the crown prince wanted to go his own way. "Out with Calle" might well mean he was out on a date. For it was now that girls came into his life in a big way.

However his first kiss was not at Sigtuna. It took place in 1952 with the Danish princess Anne-Marie, the king's cousin, Nenne informs us. The shameless young man was all of five or six years old. Although some suspect

55

that Anne-Marie (now married to Constantine, ex-king of Greece) may have been the instigator.

Parties at Hum were not exactly trend-setters. There were school dances and afternoons left free for polonaise and ring dance- in Sunday best and compulsory gym shoes. The absolute pits for most Hum students but it was the only entertainment there was, so under duress they would acquiesce to the ordeal.

In Sigtuna one free port of call was the home of his classmate Michael Odevall. Michael's parents enjoyed having young peo-

Confirmation at Borgholm Church on Öland. The whole family were there, represented here by his mother Sibylla and King Gustav VI Adolf, as well as 10 000 curious onlookers.
SVENSKT PRESSFOTO 1962

What did you get for history? The crown prince comparing grades with fellow students Carl Banér, Sven Olaf Rapp, Svante Martinsson and Peter Udén.
SYDSVENSKAN 1960

The Swedish succession is cognastic rather than agnastic. This means the eldest child of the head of state is heir to the throne, whether male or female. Since the beginning of the 18th century until parliament changed the law in 1980, only a male child could be heir to the throne

Official portrait of Crown Prince Carl Gustaf on his fourteenth birthday.
WELINDER HOVFOTO 1960

A solemn crown prince Carl Gustaf swears his Oath of Allegiance to King Gustav VI Adolf at the State Opening of Parliament in The Great Hall. The oath was administered by the Justice Minister Herman Kling.
REPORTAGEBILD 1965

ple around the house and more or less held open house for their son's friends. Incidentally Michael Odevall is still one of the king's closest friends and works in the Foreign Office as press attaché in Sweden's permanent commission at the United Nations in New York. The crown prince shared rooms first in Aludden (Alder Point) House and later in Herrgården (Manor) House with Carl Banér and Carl Johan Smith. Homework was compulsory every weekday evening from 17.30 to 19.30. Lights out in the rooms varied by age, but in upper school was 21.45. Students were allowed one home leave a month, although the crown prince with official engagements would go more often.

Romance rumours? The tabloids were full of them during his Sigtuna years. One day it would be Ulla Klang, the daughter of an attendant at the school; next Lill-Anna Jansson; then Titti Wachtmeister; and for a while Pia Degermark, who went to a school nearby. Later Leena Skog popped up.

– The king has always loved blondes, his schoolmates tell us.

But in a 1967 interview the crown prince confessed with some embarrassement:

– I like independent women. I don't really go for the sweet fair-haired types. If I must express a preference then it is for brunettes.

His choice of a wife hardly contradicts this!

58

Mottos of the Swedish Kings:

Carl XVI Gustaf: *För Sverige —i tiden*   (For Sweden – in keeping with the times)
Gustav VI Adolf: *Plikten framför allt*   (Duty Above All)
Gustav V: *Med folket för fosterlandet*   (With The People For Our Country)
Oskar II: *Brödrafolkens väl*   (For The Good of Our Sister Nations)

Idyllic scene from the 60s. Grandfather the King and Crown Prince Carl Gustaf out for an afternoon stroll among many others in the grounds of Drottningholm palace. The idea of bodyguards had yet to be invented.
PHOTO: LENNART NILSSON 1965

White student hat at last. Schoolmates throw a happy Tjabbe into the air outside Sigtuna Academy of Liberal Arts at his high school graduation on 22 April 1966.
PHOTO: RONNY KARLSSON 1966

"Sjungom studentens lyckliga dag" (Let's sing the praises of the student's happy day) is Sweden's "official" student song, composed by Prince Gustav (1827-52), Duke of Uppland. Prince Gustav was the second son of Oskar I and also composed the well-known songs *"Glad såsom fågeln"* (Happy as a Bird) and *"I rosens doft"* (In The Scent of a Rose). The lyrics to all three songs are by Herman Sätherberg.

Lots and lots of kisses of congratulations to a happy student prince at his reception in the Yellow Room at the Palace in Stockholm, following the celebrations in Sigtuna. Blondes are to the fore.
SYDSVENSKAN 1966

Man of the world. A Swedish Crown Prince Comes To London. *SVENSKT PRESSFOTO 1965*

His confirmation must not be forgotten. The ceremony was conducted in Borgholm on Öland by Archbishop Gunnar Hultgren. A crowd of 10 000 well-wishers were waiting outside in the square.

In 1965 Queen Louise, Ist to Sibylla's family, passed away. The widowed King Gustav VI Adolf received a letter of sympathy from a seven year old schoolboy.

– Your majesty should not be sad. Your majesty still has his prince.

And in numerous interviews since then "his prince" has confirmed that his grandfather was indeed at this time his best friend.

It is anybody's guess how many people crowded into the schoolyard in Sigtuna when Tjabbe graduated from high school on 22 April 1966. But it was packed to overflowing.

It was the happiest celebration in little Sigtuna's history and it ran on well into the second day. All the family were there, with his grandfather the king in the lead and a proud and relieved mother Sibylla alongside.

The happy prince was showered with flowers and submitted manfully to frequent photo opportunities as one old flame after another from his Sigtuna years placed their kisses for the cameras.

But the bubble burst when the media published his grades. The crown prince was not amused. Assorted professors paraded before the cameras to question in their most melancholy tone whether grades that included a straight C and a B warranted an overall pass in the Studenten.

Anyway for the record here are the actual grades: Swedish Ba, English Ba, German B, French B?, Christianity Ba, Philosophy Ba, Sociology Ba, History Ba, Geography AB, Mathematics C, Biology Ba, Physics B, Chemistry B, Drawing Ba, Music B, Gymnastics AB, Behaviour A, Orderliness A. At that time one was allowed to fail one subject if other subjects made up for it or a good account of oneself was given in orals. But a 'B?' for French was clearly not a good grade and there were experts who with hindsight declared they would never pass somebody with these grades.

But now Tjabbe had his white student hat and nobody was going to take it away from him. He was given a gold watch by his mother who also put on a student ball at the palace for 167 guests. Cecilia Lewenhaupt from Geddesholm – Noppe's elder sister – escorted the crown prince into dinner and there was rocking and rolling like never before on the parquet floor of the palace.

The student prince now had until 1st June to party and loaf about, celebrating his 20th birthday along the way. For this he received a car of his own for the first time in his life, a light blue Volvo P1800. The youth of today will not understand its significance. But let us just say it was the same car Roger Moore drove in his role as The Saint!

Then back to reality. Recruit 460430-001 was drafted into the navy for his two years of national service. Meanwhile nine eminent gentlemen began to brood over the form of the crown prince's further education.

1966 and the crown prince begins his naval officer's training, here learning to climb the rigging. *PHOTO: BERT OLSSON 1966*

JUST LIKE ANY OTHER YOUNG MAN.

Now they would make a king out of Tjabbe. Nine wise men – only men – were appointed to organise his education and make a man of Carl Gustaf, something he seems to have managed perfectly well by himself.

The nine were Prince Bertil, Sibylla's chamberlain and head of IBM Gösta Lewenhaupt an old friend of the crown prince's father, Chartered Engineer Bo Ekelund, Major General Malcolm Murray, University Chancellor Nils Gustav Rosén, Major Hans Skiöldebrand, Baron Hans Beck-Friis, Chartered Economist Lennart Ekelund and Lieutenant-Colonel Harold Smith.

In the background were Admiral Stig H:son Ericson, Chief Governor of the Royal Palaces Allan Nordenstam, the head of the Cellulosa concern Eje Mossberg and the rector of Stockholm University Håkan Nial. The crown prince was given a racing start with two and a half years of army, navy and air force training with emphasis on the navy. He began with a round-the-world voyage aboard H.M.S. Älvsnabben, a wonderful but tightly guarded journey, the official bulletins reporting that dashing Naval Recruit 001 was being treated just like any other young man, knocking off rust, cleaning toilets and peeling potatoes like everybody else.

The moment H.M.S. Älvsnabben docked however, the naval recruit changed into Sweden's Crown Prince. Aides arrived, journalists surrounded him and bodyguards escorted him to embassy parties and gala dinner engagements. When he arrived in Hobart Tasmania for instance, Lord and Lady Gardiner invited him to a reception at their charming palace where a game of indoor cricket was organised on the enormous marble floors of the Hall of Mirrors in the early hours of the morning.

In Honolulu he was welcomed by the beautiful dark-haired Rose-Marie Alvarez, who draped the obligatory garland of flowers around Tjabbe's neck. The picture of the handsome shirt-sleeved sailor garlanded with flowers flashed around the world. Otherwise he was just like everyone else.

When Naval Recruit 001 The Prince returned to Sweden in 1967 after his long voyage on H.M.S.Älvsnabben he was given an intensive course in each branch of the armed services. He went to Karlberg, studied flying in Uppsala, did some advanced naval training at Näsby Park and went on courses at

Ordinary Seaman Carl Gustaf celebrating his 21st birthday in the navy aboard H.M.S. Älvsnabben on his fascinating round-the-world voyage 1966-67. At the time the age of majority was 21 for everyone except the king who was required by the constitution to wait until he was 25 and worthy to inherit the crown.
PHOTO: KJELL JOHANSSON 1967

Sweden's Military Academy. He took his naval officer exams in 1968. He flew fighter planes, bivouaced high in the Swedish fells, ate pea soup from a mess-tin, sailed with the training ships Gladan (Kite) and Falken (Falcon) and parachuted from the top of the Karlsborg training tower, with a safety

Another port. Another embrace? Beautiful Rose-Marie Alvarez welcomes H.M.S. Älvsnabben and the Crown Prince of Sweden to Hawaii where the sun always shines.
PRESSENS BILD 1967

wire attached just in case.

–A surprisingly good jump declared the experts.

He was a lieutenant four times over: in the Swedish Lifeguards, the Jämtland light infantry, the Royal Swedish Navy and the RoyalSwedish Air Force, a normal step in a military career. Later on he would be Colonel-in-Chief of two regiments and the head of Sweden's armed forces.

In 1968 the crown prince took an apartment with Michael Odevall and an aide on Luthagsesplanaden in Uppsala to begin academic studies at the university.

The idea was not for the crown prince to take a degree or sit written exams. The nine wise men thought the crown prince needed to get his nose into some practical subjects and familiarise himself with subjects such as sociology, political science, fiscal law and economics.

Tjabbe enjoys himself at Uppsala in the same ways as any other student. He discusses "life" and Third World problems into the early hours, turns up at student corridor parties and the more formal events organised by the student unions – but only dances with women he knows, we are told. His best friends protect him from overattentive admirers. And he abandons the use of titles and says quite simply "I am Carl Gustaf".

In 1970 Sibylla's ex-chancellor Gösta Lewenhaupt who had been keeping a watchful eye on the crown prince ever since he was a child carries out an appraisal of Carl Gustaf. Files in the Bernadotte Library tell us that he found "admirable traits" in the young man's character:

"He has overcome the shyness he inherited at birth.

His conversation is pleasant and natural.

He is blessed with great strength – his friends choose not to fight him.

He is naturally polite, a trait common to all Bernadottes.

He has moderation in spiritual and material things.

He is very sensible with money.

He is a loyal friend and an honest man.

He is extremely sensitive to the ways of the modern world.

He is well aware of his duty."

What a fine fellow!

But how much better if after Uppsala the royal education were complemented with a programme exploring some of the ways of modern Swedish society. So he visits government departments and local authorities, industries, factories, laboratories and schools. He studies the law courts, social organisa-

After advancing on motorbike from Varberg, the crown prince as head of an artillery company defends the lovely bathing beaches of the Örby meadows outside Hälsingborg against a mock invasion
PHOTO: OLA SVENSSON 1967

How many guards does a king manage to inspect during his lifetime? Here in a row is one of them. Crown Prince Carl Gustaf with the English admiral Donough O'Brian at his side inspecting the visiting English fleet in Stockholm.
PHOTO: FREDDY LINDSTRÖM 1971

tions and institutions, trade unions and employer federations. Special emphasis is being given to government, parliament and the education department, insists the Palace.

He gains work experience with SKF, Göteborgs-Posten, SCA and Facit, inspects the guard and pays a call on U Thant in New York. But these are not the only things going on, there are frequent trips to the night club Alexandra's, holidays in foreign parts and a motor rally in Monte Carlo.

In 1972 the crown prince sets off for the Olympic Games in Munich where he happens to meet a nice young hostess with a flair for languages...

In the 70s the age of majority for ordinary Swedish citizens was 21 but the heir to the throne had to wait until he was 25, before he was allowed to carry out royal duties in his grandfather's absence.

"Herewith Princess Sibylla can consider that her duties as the royal guardian have been brought to a happy and successful conclusion, allowing her to turn her attention to her own affairs." So wrote Gunnar Unger in Svenska Dagbladet. But her time was short. In 1972 the crown prince's mother dies of cancer. Her last official appearance is at King Gustav Adolf's 90th birthday a few weeks before her death.

This is followed by the dramatic events of the late summer of 1973 with Gustav VI Adolf's long struggle against illness at Helsingborg Infirmary, coinciding with the dra-

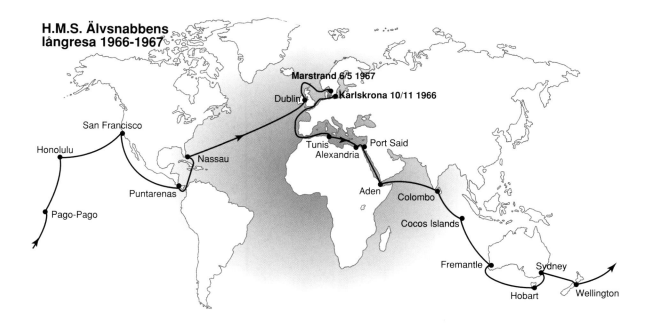

H.M.S. Älvsnabbens
långresa 1966-1967

Marstrand 6/5 1967

Karlskrona 10/11 1966

Dublin

San Francisco

Honolulu

Nassau

Puntarenas

Pago-Pago

Tunis
Alexandria

Port Said

Aden

Colombo

Cocos Islands

Fremantle

Sydney

Hobart

Wellington

Next inspection, though in a lighter mood. Sigtuna high school graduate and Uppsala undergraduate Bernadotte being presented with brooms instead of arms at the annual dinner of the Lund naval officers' club. *PHOTO: JAN DAHLANDER 1968*

The never-ending pictures of the crown prince partying gave republicans much grist for their mill and
led to the monarchy being under threat for many
years. At this dinner at Lund's Grand Hotel Carl
Gustaf is enjoying the company of Vivi Lodding.
PHOTO: JAN DAHLANDER 1968

The crown prince's first press conference took place in his student rooms on Luthagsesplanaden in Uppsala in 1968.
PHOTO: BOSSE JOHANSSON 1968

There is something about a sailor. The king's 21st birthday contin-
ued with a party in Dublin where the fair-haired Elisabeth
Lundström is being told the full story about the exciting voyage of
H.M.S. Älvsnabben. *PHOTO: KJELL JOHANSSON 1967*

A fair-haired maiden of a more mature and stable model: Provincial Governor Gösta Netzén's betrothed Marianne Hamilton taking a whirl on the dance floor with the crown prince at Knutsgillet in Malmö.
PHOTO: LASSE SVENSSON 1973

Whispering sweet nothings in Pia Degermark's ear.
AP 1968

One beautiful fair-haired young lady who moved in royal circles for several years was Pia Degermark. At this time, at her own student party, she was already a star after the film director Bo Widerberg had discovered her in a photograph dancing with the crown prince two years previously.
SYDSVENSKAN 1968

Next to be treated to the crown prince's dancing skills is Margareta Olsson at the Lund naval officers club.
PHOTO: JAN DAHLANDER 1968

**Prepare the way for The Lord... A new king celebrates the beginning of
Advent in Lund Cathedral with Churchwarden Sven Håkan Ohlsson.**
PHOTO: STAFFAN HAGBLOM 1973

ma in Stockholm's Norrmalmstorg and the final days of that year's parliamentary elec-
tions. The country seems to be grinding to a
halt as news of the outcome of the hostage
drama is awaited with the same anxiety as
Gunnar Biörck's bulletins from the hospital
steps.

When the news of the old king's death comes on 15 September, the night before the
election, a wave of sympathy wells up for Carl
Gustaf, who automatically becomes king
when his grandfather breathes his dying breath. At 27 he is the world's youngest monarch. His grandfather was nearly 68 when

he became king. Formally Carl XVI Gustaf
ascends the throne on 19 September 1973
when he swears his royal oath before the Justice Minister Lennart Geijer, announces his
royal name and motto and makes his first
speech as king, the address from the throne,
the various ceremonies taking place in the
council chamber and in the Great Hall.

Crowds gather on Norrbro and Lejonbacken to cheer the new king. With Prince
Bertil alongside him he waves to the crowds
from the palace balcony, pleased and much
moved by the adulation. He chooses as his
motto: 'För Sverige – i tiden' (For Sweden –

In March 1973 Crown Prince Carl Gustaf visited the Malmö offices of Sydsvenskan and is seen here reading Kvällsposten fresh off the presses.
PHOTO: TORBJÖRN CARLSON 1973

The king shall be "of the true faith", which means baptised into the Swedish Church. Princes and princesses are to be brought up in that same faith, according to the Act of succession.

On his visit to Sydsvenskan the crown prince met three generations of Wahlgrens who were a strong influence on the newspaper for many years. Alongside the crown prince is Major Christer Wahlgren, chairman of the board, followed by his grandson Christer. On the far right is the managing editor at that time, Olof Wahlgren.
PHOTO: BERT OLSSON 1973

The crown prince in conversation with Prime Minister Olof Palme after his first cabinet meeting. The king came to be a great admirer of Olof Palme, so much so that following his murder in 1986 the king ordered the palace flag to be flown at half mast, an honour traditionally reserved for the royal family.
PHOTO: FREDDY LINDSTRÖM 1971

In September 1971 Crown Prince Carl Gustaf presided over his first cabinet meeting deputising for his grandfather Gustav Adolf VI who was in Italy with an archaeological expedition at the time. A minister's position at the cabinet table depends on length of service, the newest ministers sitting at the foot of the table furthest from the king.
At the cabinet table on the left: Cabinet Minister Carl Lidbom, Bengt Norling, Sven Moberg, Alva Myrdal, Sven Aspling, Rune Johansson, Gunnar Sträng and Olof Palme (hidden). On the right: Ingvar Carlsson, Bertil Löfberg, Ingemund Bengtsson, Lennart Geijer, Sven-Eric Nilsson, Eric Holmqvist and Krister Wickman.
PHOTO: FREDDY LINDSTRÖM 1971

These are the King's constitutional duties:
The King is the head of state.
The King presides at the special cabinet meetings convened on a change of government.
The King presides at the informatory cabinet meetings attended by members of the government.
The King opens parliament in October each year.
The King is chairman of the parliament's foreign affairs advisory council elected
for consultations between the parliament and the government on foreign affairs.
The King holds the highest military rank and is colonel-in-chief of several regiments.
Sweden's armed forces are however under the sole command of the government.
The King receives the Letters of Credence of foreign envoys.
The King signs the Letters of Credence of Swedish envoys.

They may already be in love. This is earliest known picture of Carl Gustaf and Silvia together, but in Sweden it only came to light after the photographer Bertil Jigert had taken his "first" of the couple in a Porsche on Öland. When the Öland picture was published the media searched their files and found this one by a German magazine.
BILDZEITUNG 1972

Grandfather and grandson. King Gustav Adolf VI could be strict and make heavy demands on his grandson, but they got on extremely well despite the 64-year age difference. In interviews the crown prince explained that his grandfather was his best friend.
SYDSVENSKAN 1971

Nowadays the king pays taxes and declares his income each year like any other Swedish citizen.

If the king is abroad or ill his duties can be delegated with first choice being always the member of the royal house who is over 18 and heir to the throne, Crown Princess Victoria at present.

This would not be allowed today 25 years on. Crown Prince Carl Gustaf dressed up as a negro and smoking a cigar at Åre Carnival.
PHOTO: BENGT WEILERT 1971

Carl Gustaf's first moments as king late in the evening on 15 September 1973. Just before this picture was taken the old king Gustav VI Adolf had died at Helsinborg Infirmary. Marshal of the Realm Stig H:son Ericson came out onto the hospital steps to announce: "The king is dead! Long live the king!" Shortly afterwards a pale and sombre Carl Gustaf emerged as the new king followed by Princess Christina. From the waiting media came a spontaneous cheer for King Carl XVI Gustaf who stood deeply moved holding his big sister Titti's hand.
PHOTO: PER LINDSTRÖM 1973

The new king leaves Helsingborg Infirmary followed to his car by photographers and members of the public. These are dramatic times in Sweden with the people going to the polls the next day.
PHOTO: PER LINDSTRÖM 1973

The morning after his grandfather's death, King Carl Gustaf arrived at Bromma by air from Skåne and was given flowers by this little girl. He was met by ministers in mourning including Prime Minister Olof Palme and Finance Minister Gunnar Sträng. The election results were counted on the Sunday evening and resulted in a hung parliament with 175 Conservative seats and 175 for the Social Democrats. Many expected a change of government with the Social Democrats losing power, but it was thought that the death of King Gustav VI Adolf influenced the outcome, many voting for the government. In uncertain times people tend to vote for stability. In the next election in 1976 the Social Democrats were thrown out.
PHOTO: JAN DELDEN 1973

1/125th of a second

– Beware of the Hacks!

King Gustav VI Adolf never gave interviews.

– He may have given Vecko-Journalen an interview once, suggests Elisabeth Tarras-Wahlberg, head of information at the Palace.

When Carl Gustaf became king in 1973 the Palace did not have a press and information office along today's lines. Help was available for a couple of hours a week from either the Press Liaison Officer Sten Egnell, retired editor-in-chief of Nerikes Allehanda and the trade publication Läder & Skor (Leather & Shoes) or from the king's secretary Carl-Fredrik Palmstierna.

With the resurgence of the left and the events of '68 uppermost in the media's collective mind, interest in the royal family was virtually non-existent. Dagen Nyheter's coverage of King Gustav VI Adolf's 90th birthday in 1972 was a case in point. Before the event there was not a single article published on the subject. On the day itself the only mention was an article about the complaints of coin dealers and collectors regarding the qualiy of the commemorative issue. Otherwise there was a tiny article on the presents pouring in for the aging monarch and somewhat grudgingly a route map for the royal procession.

There was a wave of protest! Readers telephoned DN to complain. THE KING was NINETY. Surely this was worth writing about, said the enraged public. The editors backed off, admitted their mistake and did their best to make amends. Seven photographers and five journalists including the legendary Jan-Olof Olsson (Jolo) were sent around town to get a feel for the historic occasion. In DN the next day there were quite a few articles and a gigantic front.page picture.

A pair of excited English photographers trying hard for the perfect picture of the six-year old crown prince in his beloved pedal car.
IBL 1952

After this, DN reporters understood that they should feel in their bones the Swedish public's real and genuine affection for the royal family and that this was sacrosanct.

But several years later after the old king's death, Sten Egnell was still annoyed with the media. He thought they should be constrained, because all they ever did was stalk the new king at discotheques. The instinct of the Palace was that the less said the better. Their motto was "Beware of The Hacks!" Once bitten, twice shy.

During his student years and later when training, thousands of pictures of the smoking, drinking and partying crown prince and king were published both here at home and abroad.

A never.ending parade of fast cars, boats and women. One affair after another was how the rumours went. The all-time low was reached in 1974 when Fib-Aktuellt published an article entitled 'The King's Harem' where several female acquaintances of the king were named and described as "girls who Carl Gustaf knew would not stoop so low as to gossip about their 'nights of passion with the king'".

Goodness knows how often King Carl Gustaf has been hugged in his time. Here a florist Asta Olsson in Växjö takes the chance to hug the king and advertise her firm with a big pretty bouquet for the king.
PHOTO: ALF WEIHED 1975

The young ladies were part of the king's circle of friends (many of them still are) and had all been previously associated with him as "old flames": Barbro Ehn, Liv Porjé, Charlotte Klingspor, Ankie Christenson, Titti Wachtmeister etc.

Everyone was absolutely furious, the king himself, the palace and many of the king's friends who were cited in the article as providing him with "sleep-over places". It is extremely unusual for the palace to retaliate against the media.

– It feels terrible each time the king is ambushed by the media. Nobody, not the palace, nor the king, nor anyone else, can go out and put the record straight, a close friend of the king observed recently.

But in the Fib-Aktuellt case both the king and the young ladies mentioned did want to hit back.

The marshal of the realm Stig H:son Ericson approached the press ombudsman, Lennart Groll who considered taking up the matter with the press complaints commission. But further action was avoided when Lukas Bonnier, Managing Director of Åhléns & Åkerlund intervened to give the king a written apology deeply regretting the article and implying that heads would roll at Fib-Aktuellt. This together with letters of apology to those involved was enough to satisfy everybody.

Today one of the young ladies named in the article, Ankie Ramberg (née Christenson), is a successful lawyer and a member of the press complaints commission!

The following year 1975 another unique media incident took place when an appeal to the media from the palace was sent out by the wire service TT. It described how the king had noticed "with growing indignation" the intense media coverage and the creative articles of recent weeks, both in Sweden and abroad, regarding the king's skiing vacation in Switzerland, the reported gift of an icon and rumours of a forthcoming engagement.

– We regard it as entirely proper to appeal to the Swedish media to tone down their coverage of the king's private life and his personal friends, the Palace emphasised in the TT-telegram.

Clearly the time had come to improve the relationship between the king and the media and the Palace had decided to try a completely different approach. The foreign office's head of information Jan Mårtenson was taken on full time. He became head of the Palace's private office and was given the task of solving the media problem.

Jan Mårtenson thought that a new king in a new age needed to be less reactive and more outgoing in his handling of the media. The Swedish people had a right to know more about the monarchy and how the king functioned within that monarchy. Full openness was to be the order of the day. But in return the media – and the Swedish people – should respect the king's privacy.

How this has worked out everybody knows who has followed the media over the past 20 years: the king's wedding, the birth of his children, the children's schooling (and confirmation camps), colds, claims of cosmetic surgery, and teenage romances – all have been reported in minute detail.

Mårtenson was given a flying start dealing with all the Silvia rumours and later the engagement and the royal wedding in 1976. The weekly glossy magazines that were in a serious circulation crisis at the time were already celebrating the engagement between Silvia and Carl Gustaf with champagne at their editorial offices and rapidly called in extra staff. This would get the circulation up! The Swedish love of royalty after lying fallow for several years, would blossom once more before the prospect of future royal children and – even fur-

Cover boy for the glossy monthly Z, no.1–2, 1988. "King, Girls – and Indians!"

The picture that really set the romance rumours buzzing around Olympic Games hostess Silvia Sommerlath. The photographer Bertil Jigert took the picture of Silvia and the king on Öland, visited by Silvia in great secrecy in the summer of 1973. Jigert knew the crown prince had a party for his friends at Solliden and he also knew that they normally took a ride down to the beach for a swim the following morning. So the next morning he chose a strategic spot, Hotel Strand in Borgholm, sat down and waited. Before long sure enough along came the crown prince's car with his beloved in the front seat and Jigert took his dream picture without the young people noticing. The young couple managed to hold their relationship secret (well...!) for four years before eventually announcing their engagement at the Royal Palace in Stockholm on 12 March 1976.
PHOTO: BERTIL JIGERT 1973

It just went click said the king to reporters at the press conference announcing his engagement in March 1776 when describing how he had fallen in love with the Olympic Games hostess Silvia Sommerlath. And they certainly look very much in love.
PHOTO: FREDDY LINDSTRÖM 1976

ther into the future – new romances, weddings and babies. At least so the weekly glossies saw the future.

In 1976 the media poured into Stockholm for the royal wedding with hundreds of journalists being accredited. Jan Mårtenson stuck to his policy of openness, but warned the media to respect the royal couple's private lives. But with regard to the biggest secret of all – where they would go for their honeymoon – the Palace remained very tight-lipped. After the wedding the Palace was swamped with phone calls and written requests to interview the new queen.

Mårtenson soon needed reinforcements. In 1979 Elisabeth Tarras-Wahlberg was taken on as his part-time press assistant. She

was soon full time as Jan Mårtenson left later in the year to become an assistant secretary general at the UN. Today the Palace's press office has grown. Elisabeth Tarras-Wahlberg is head of information and leads a team of three: Catherine Broms, Cecilia Wilmhardt and Göran Alm. They write the king's speeches, arrange state visits and other trips, reply to invitations and letters, coordinate TV-camera shots and so on. They also service the many other needs of the media and the public for information: How many windows are there in the palace? When was Madeleine born? Can we have a picture of Drottningholm for the gingerbread house we are baking? How many Bernadotte kings have there been? and so on.

Jan Mårtenson, head of the Palace's private office and responsible for media relations was the first full-time holder of the job. Here he is trying to organise the world's press with the help of a rolled-up magazine. The royal couple held their first joint press conference at Solliden on their return from their honeymoon.
SYDSVENSKAN 1976

Married at last. The 1976 wedding of the year as Carl Gustaf and Silvia leave the altar and proceed out of the church followed by bridesmaids and pages. Outside 150 000–180 000 people line the route of the royal procession cheering and throwing confetti.
PHOTO: JACOB FORSELL 1976

The kiss that hundreds of TV cameras and photographers missed, although not Expressen's Jonny Graan. He describes what happened:
– I took up my position in an apartment opposite the church meaning to take pictures of the newly-weds when they came out after the service. I was there in good time, well before Silvia and Carl Gustaf arrived at the church. Suddenly I caught sight of them passing the armoury on their way to the church, and it was here the bridegroom took his opportunity. It was only for a second but it was long enough for me to focus my camera and take my life's picture.
The picture was unique. Almost certainly the only picture of the royal couple exchanging tokens of affection in public.
PHOTO: JONNY GRAAN 1976

91

Guess which Swedish royal event provides the biggest pile of press cuttings for the Palace archives each year. Swedish Farming Week! This is the week the king awards milk prizes to Swedish farmers. So every rural newspaper diligently publishes the names and pictures of the local prize winners photographed with the king. That fills column after column!

There have been a few occasions in recent years when the Palace has protested against impertinent media coverage of the royal family. Marshal of the Realm Per Sköld complained about a radio piece by a freelance writer Jens Ganman in the young peoples programme "Signal" in 1994, for instance, when he accosted Prince Carl Philip at his confirmation camp. Sköld's argument was that the feature's "sole purpose was to belittle Prince Carl Philip". Sköld won his case. The radio and TV Complaints Committee condemned the programme on the grounds that at Carl Philip's young age it "represented an incursion into his private life that could not be justified by any overwhelming public interest".

92

It is always like this whenever the king does anything: the general public, photographers and officials. Not even here was the king left in peace. But perhaps he caught a salmon on the first day of the salmon fishing season in Mörrumsån.

PHOTO: JAN ASPLUND 1973

A fine pair of legs!
PHOTO: ANDERS HOLMSTRÖM 1991

An even finer pair of legs!

– A quick word, Carl Gustaf...

The act of 1974 defined the duties and functions of the monarch. It is one of four constitutional acts, the others being the 1810 Act of Succession, the 1949 Freedom of the Press Act and the 1991 Freedom of Speech Act.

The royal birthdays:

King Carl Gustaf Folke Hubertus,
30 April 1946
Queen Silvia Renate,
23 December 1943
Crown Princess Victoria Ingrid
Alice Désirée, Duchess of
Västergötland, 14 July 1977
Princess Madeleine Thérèse Amelie
Josephine, Duchess of Hälsingland
and Gästrikland,
10 June 1982
Prince Carl Philip Edmund Bertil,
Duke of Värmland, 13 May 1979

The king is never pictured with a cigarette nowadays although he smokes in private. Trying to give up of course by alternating Nicorette with cigarettes.
PHOTO: RONNY JOHANSSON 1967

How are relations between the media and the royal family today?

There are as many answers as there are journalists.

– During the 90s the media has established a symbiotic relationship with the royal family. The servility, particularly on TV, is worrying and disgraceful writes Aftonbladet journalist Anette Kullenberg, for instance.

– Why such a bowing and scraping should develop in a democracy with such complete freedom of speech as we have in Sweden is hard to understand, she continues.

Yet leaving aside the weekly glossy magazines and their gluttonous appetites for everything royal, be it divorces of friends of the royal couple, Silvia's beautiful hair–dos or Victoria's dream prince to do a quick sweep through royal coverage in the daily press, we find this "bowing and scraping" line seems difficult to sustain.

Reporting of the royal couple's various appearances – to the extent such reports exist at all – can be characterised as anything from weary indifference (inaugurations) to frenzied attacks (Ulf Nilson in Expressen, Anette Kullenberg in Aftonbladet).

Since it is difficult to get an interview with the king – he gives perhaps two or three a year and only on subjects that he finds suitable – reporters are restricted to either group interviews in disorganised settings, such as hunts in the forest or during brief interludes during hectic state visits, or to interviewing those close to the king. Journalists also know the king does not comment on current affairs with a political dimension. If such questions are asked he either answers vaguely or responds with the words "I cannot comment on that". Try as one might one will always be met with a disapproving look and evasive phrases. Nonetheless at the Bergslag Hunt in the autumn of 1995 one journalist tried to force his way through the wall of "How many elks has his Majesty shot in his life?" to ask the king what he thought about the Mona Sahlin affair which had just blown up.

– I had to ask the question, muttered the journalist later, after the king had quite properly given an evasive response.

It is important to emphasize that there is nothing either in the constitution or anywhere else that forbids the king from saying anything he wants. But King Carl Gustaf has adopted the policy of his tactful grandfather, avoiding any involvement in day to day debates and in particular in party political issues. But his views can still be known. Norwegian seal hunting, bringing up children, joining the European Union. There are plenty of occasions when the king does speak out.

When the king was on a visit to the EU in Brussels in 1995, a press conference was arranged for a group of experienced Swedish journalists. Foreign Trade Minister Mats Hall-ström, the EU ambassador Frank Belfrage, secretary to the Cabinet Jan Eliasson and others sat on the king's side of the table.

As a reporter one expects a couple of interesting remarks on such occasions. If the king has nothing of his own to say then his experts advise him in advance on what to say. And there is nothing wrong with saying it with emphasis and conviction. But in Brussels it was mostly courtesies. The king thought the visit was "interesting", "it is important that Sweden participates in the work of European cooperation" and "it is important to push for greater openness and less bureaucracy".

Amidst such a morass of evasions and unfinished sentences one really must read ones notes very carefully to find something worth homing in on. Reports back to editorial offices said the king had pleaded for more equality and less bureaucracy in the EU, had taken up the question of the labour market situation and so on. Uncontroversial and "safe". The palace thought everything had gone "well". But the journalists were disappointed. They know that although the king has to perform a balancing act between what he can and cannot say, even so the most mundane statement can be made to sound convincing. Just listen to the politicians!

– Regrettably the king is not a media person, his friends explain. You journalists always expect answers to be verbally well-oiled and intellectually coherent and have been spoilt by this. Swedes do not actually talk like that. And nor does the king.

On state visits the royal couple travel around and get to see and get to know many interesting things. The media are more than welcome to accompany them, but are often kept away when it gets really interesting.

When the king was on a state visit to Germany in 1993, for instance, and visited a refuse disposal facility in Bonn, the media were forced to stand around outside the gates while the king and his party were being given an interesting lecture on Bonn's programme for citizens to sort their refuse into different colour barrels and sacks. This was something ex-

citing and topical for journalists to report, but they were not allowed to hear the lectures so coverage could easily have ended up with the rather mundane throw–away line: "later the king visited a recycling centre".

On this occasion a Bonn journalist explained the waste recycling to the Swedish reporters at the factory gate and so the Swedish media were fed reports of the exciting project after all.

But it was the same thing when the royal couple visited an art gallery. The Curator guided the royal couple around explaining about the fascinating works of art. Yet journalists were made to keep their distance and so they heard nothing. If a policy of openness allows journalists to accompany the royal couple on state visits then they ought to receive the same information as the royal couple. That way the media coverage of the king would be more meaningful than reports of the colour of the queen's hat or of what flags were flying.

Royal theatre, tradition and pomp are all very well but are much better when served up alongside a few essential and interesting facts. Comparisons are made with royal reporters in neighbouring countries, in particular the British with their rather breathless reporting about royalty, and how the rather more reserved treatment of the Bernadotte family by the Swedish media compares. On occasions we Swedish journalists are amazed at our foreign colleagues.

On one occasion during the German state visit the royal couple were answering questions at a press conference held at some knightly hall along the way. Asking the queen how she keeps her clothes nice and how she and the king keep themselves smart is fine. But Swedish journalists had to gasp at the German journalist's next question:

– Doesn't the queen ever sweat?

What journalist would ever dream of asking the prime minister, the governor of the Bank of Sweden or Carola a question like that?

98

Who complained about the king's lack of spontaneity? Here he is cheering for his country at a hockey match during the Winter Olympics in Lillehammar, together with Queen Silvia and the Norwegian royal couple Sonja and Harald. In front of the royal dignitaries sits the then Deputy Finance Minister Bo Lundgren. Behind are bodyguards.
PHOTO: ANDERS WIKLUND 1994

THE KING AND HIS ROYAL GAFFES.

When King Carl Gustaf visited Falun in 1973 he signed his name on the rock wall of the mine. It came out as Cal Gustf. Shortly afterwards in cabinet the king forgot to thank the departing ministers Camilla Odhnoff, Krister Wickman and Sven Moberg.

Since then each royal gaffe has been dutifully reported by the press. Slips of the tongue, unfortunate and controversial remarks, outright blunders – all are preserved. In most press archives there is a file of the king's "unfortunate remarks" or "gaffes". Hardly anybody else in public life has one.

The list of royal gaffes is extensive:

– Men are better monarchs than women, the king commented at a press conference in Seattle for foreign reporters in 1982.

– A woman is more sensitive and has stronger family ties, he added.

Before that he had said that women better stick to bringing up children. On one occasion the king said about caning:

– I don't think it helps to hit children. They get frightened and can get angry and hit back.

He became a friend of the anti-nuclear lobby when he said he disliked opening nuclear power stations, but did so if he had to.

And he had the sex equality lobby against him when he explained that the communists were his friends since they had voted against allowing female heirs to the throne. The king's comments on Norwegian seal hunting was nearly enough to start a war between Norway and Sweden.

– If Gro Harlem Brundtland cannot look after the seal problem, then I wonder how she can look after the Norwegian people, the king said when he was in New Zealand in 1989.

The Norwegians were furious and filled their newspapers with stories of how the Swedish king roared around in his speedboat scaring the lives out of the seal colonies in the Baltic or shot poor defenseless elks on his royal hunts. But the king refused to withdraw his remark and became a hero to environmentalists.

He has spoken out in favour of grades in school and entry into the EU and talked about burns at a Ronneby conference all about lockjaw.

He says Norrbotten when he is in Västerbotten, Uppsala when he is in Lund and addresses the good people of Örebro when he

How many overalls must a king put on in his official life? On his "Eriksgatan" journeys in Skåne the king visited Felix in Eslöv wearing this hat and a white coat. *PHOTO: TORBJÖRN ANDERSSON 1975*

It's easy for the pen to slip on a rock wall. It ended up as Cal Gustf when the king signed his name on an old copper mine in Falun. The wrong spelling was duly reported by the press.
PHOTO: ÖRJAN BJÖRKDAL 1973

is in Arboga. And the Palace denies, corrects and blames language problems whenever the king is abroad. The king tries hard to avoid making gaffes and is acutely conscious of the problem. At official functions the TV cameras are continuously focusing on his face whenever he speaks, photographers register the tiniest gesture, reporters are there with their pencils and notebooks and the public watch. Who would not be nervous and make mistakes?

Among his inner circle the king bemoans the fact that he has to sit through and listen to everybody else's gaffes but nobody worries or notes them down for posterity.

On one occasion in the beginning of the 70s when the king had spent a lot of time managing his Stenhammar estate he visited the Agricultural College in Ultuna. Accompanying him was a large entourage of learned professors and reporters. During the tour the subject of agricultural equipment and machinery came up, and the king asked about tractors with "dubbellavettage". The professor he asked had not come across the word and was confused for a moment. Immediately reporters rushed up to palace aides to find out how the king had put his foot in it this time.

– When they found out that it was the professor who was unfamiliar with the term 'lavettage' and not the king making a blunder they lost interest in writing about the inci-

The king is expected to do any daft thing the PR-men and their planning commit-
tees can think up: cut a tape; release doves and balloons, blow trombones, fire off
cannons, press start buttons etc. At the prize ceremony at the end of a sailing com-
petition in Karlskrona he had to lift up this lump of rock.
SYDÖSTRAN 1983

The king can let his hair down and be spontaneous when he feels at home, like here with the actors in the student farce "Djingis Khan" at Lund University.
PHOTO: PER LINDSTRÖM 1986

dent, explained one of his aides when giving it as an example of the media's negative attitude to the king. "Lavette" or "lavettage" was the Swedish word for gun–carriage but nowadays the term "dubbellavettage" refers to the practice of attaching an extra set of wheels to a tractor to stop it sinking into the mud.

Everyone knows about it, talks about it and sometimes writes about the fact that the king suffers from dyslexia and has reading and writing difficulties. Word blind is the term that used to be used. On occasions the king has talked about it himself. Here is a comment from the beginning of the 70s when the king said:

– I change vowels around which makes my words sound slurred.

In a 1991 interview with Dagens Nyheter he is reported to have said:

– I have no firm evidence that I am word blind. But I wonder. It has not been easy. It is a handicap for many people, he added carefully. Then he became quite animated and continued:

– As parents it is important to keep an eye open for this type of problem so that children and youngsters get training and help in time. But the most important of all is to understand their difficulties. Otherwise they may be thought dim or lazy.

The king himself did not get adequate help with his dyslexia when he was growing up. His school friends bear witness to the fact that extra lessons were given but special dyslexia training hardly ever took place during his Sigtuna years. Dyslexia or reading and writing difficulties (which mainly affect boys) are hidden handicaps which often have a neurological foundation and are genetically based. About ten per cent of the population,

Others may make mistakes but not the king.
PHOTO: TORBJÖRN ANDERSSON 1988

three children in every class, suffer from dyslexia. Today there are an estimated half a million Swedes with reading and writing disabilities of some sort. Dyslexia has nothing to do with ability and intelligence and is often associated with considerable creative ability and several other above average talents.

The author Torbjörn Lundgren, dyslexic himself and Secretary of the Association Against Reading and Writing Disabilities explains that many famous successful people confess to being dyslexic: – Lars Widding, P.C.Jersild, Eino Hanski, Jan Myrdal, Sven-Bertil Taube and Sif Ruud are a few of them and who would think of suggesting they lacked intelligence?

The problems for dyslexics vary considerably. Without going into it too deeply, typical difficulties worth mentioning are reversing rows of text, not seeing the difference between, say, b and p and seeing "den" as "ned". And when reading words wrongly "the image in the head" also goes wrong, confusing associations. Words and spelling can also be heard wrongly.

To function as an official person, make speeches, constantly listen to other people's speeches and avoid making slips of the tongue oneself when dyslexic must be a curse and a terribly heavy load to bear. It requires intense preparation, rock hard concentration and special strategies for "cracking the alphabetical code", as it is called.

– When I take the train to Karlskrona, for instance, all I see is a large K in front of me which could mean Kalmar or Karlskrona or Karlshamn for all I know. So I make sure I check the train against my ticket before getting on board, explains Torbjörn Lundgren.

Perhaps this explains why the king said Örebro instead of Arboga that time at the 550 years anniversary. Both words have the letters R, b, o and a in them. When the king said Uppsala but meant Lund perhaps he has a picture of a "university town" in his head and chose the wrong name. Nobody makes fun of the blind, the deaf or the handicapped. But everybody is free to poke fun at the king's word blindness.

When the 50th anniversary of the United Nations was celebrated in 1995 there was a live broadcast from a TV variety performance at Globen in Stockholm. The royal family was there. Siw Malmkvist came on stage dressed as Pippi Långstrump with a large sack full of gold coins.

– Hi King (Hej, kungen), she waved gladly. The audience yelled and the king waved back.

– Or is it hi Knig, (Hej knugen), Pippi repeated altering the letters around. The laughing faded away. The TV cameras zoomed in on the king and queen. And the whole of Sweden saw how they stiffened and were upset by the remark. Incidentally the real Pippi Långstrump who is a great humanist and loves people would never have made such a remark.

You can make up your own mind about how amusing it is to make fun of other people's misfortunes.

The school year 1996/97 is to be a year for the dyslexic when the Swedish Dyslexia Foundation (whose patron is Queen Silvia), the Swedish Dyslexia Association and FMLS join forces to introduce a country–wide information campaign on dyslexia.

PHOTO: PER LINDSTRÖM 1995

106

'UPPSALA says King opening a new laboratory in LUND' (Expressen).

'KING opens institute in LUND –THOUGHT HE WAS IN UPPSALA' (Kvällsposten).

PHOTO: INGEMAR D KRISTIANSEN 1995

WHEN BODSTRÖM SPOKE THE FACADE CRACKED.

On 14 January 1983 there is a meeting of the foreign affairs committee, the first after the change of government of 1982. It is a rather special occasion because there is a newly elected government so many members are there for the first time. The king is chairman as usual.

Prime minister Olof Palme has asked his new foreign secretary Lennart Bodström to brief the committee on "political developments overseas that might affect this country". Bodström is something of a pedant and takes the job awfully seriously reporting in great detail on the situation in one part of the world after another, country by country. It takes time, a lot of time.

When Bodström started into his second hour some members were having difficulty staying awake. Some rustled papers discreetely, some doodled on their agenda sheets, some fell fast asleep. Palme tried to signal Bodström to wind up, but without success. When Bodström came to the ongoing conflict in North West Senegal something happens.

The king, the chairman, takes up his agenda paper and begins to fold it. With great care and precision he folds it, presses it and smoothes out the paper until it is in a tiny little bunch. Then he begins to pull out each corner until he succeeds in making a paper propellor. He takes his pen and fixes the propellor to the point. Then he blows carefully. Surprised members see the propellor actually turn and a happy contented smile pass across the king's brow.

As far as I know this episode is unique. It is the only occasion where we find a crack in the royal facade, the only time on an official occasion that the king shed his strict formal manner and exhibited a brief instantaneous playfulness.

Otherwise his performances are always 100% correct, never diverging from the protocol and carrying out his duties with a precision which seems to touch the perfect.

Of course there are the gaffes which cause many to think him stiff and boring, pointing to Prince Bertil as a good example of how a royal person with spontaneity, humour and playfulness can lighten up the ceremonial and the formal.

But the king is ambitious, better read than many realise, duty bound and very meticulous at doing the official job of being king properly. Nearly all sources bear witness to this. But he can just as easily be relaxed and easy-going in private once he has cast off the protocol.

"The King alone shall govern the realm..." This is how the old constitution put it in the 1809 legislation, before becoming outdated by Sweden's parliamentary democratic reforms.

It is not always easy to maintain the perfect royal facade, especially when the sun is shining straight into your eyes as it did here during the king's "Eriksgata" journey in Skåne. *PHOTO: TORBJÖRN ANDERSSON 1975*

The royal couple are visiting PLM in Malmö and one of the firm's faithful old servants Velinka Spajic has the honour of presenting a bouquet of flowers.
PHOTO: BERT OLSSON 1977

In the new constitution of 1974/75 all formal political power has been taken away from the king. Already in the first paragraph of the new legislation it is clearly stated that all public power is derived from the people as represented in parliament and by the government. The king, though the country's head of state, has no formal power nowadays but retains his representative and ceremonial duties. His function is symbolic.

In the constitution there is very little about what the king should actually do. When Carl Gustaf celebrated twenty years on the throne he was thanked in particular by the Government and the Speaker for managing to fill the role of head of state in so skilful a manner.

According to the constitution the king opens parliament each year at the speaker's request and chairs the council which meets with a change of government.

The king also chairs the advisory council which meets several times a year with members of the cabinet but makes no decisions being purely advisory. Since the king fills a representative role overseas it is important he is well-informed on Swedish matters.

As head of state the king travels abroad on state visits and is host to visiting dignitaries in Sweden.

The king receives the letters of credence of foreign envoys at a ceremonial audience at the palace (full evening dress required!), holds farewell meetings with them when they return home (jacket and tie) and signs the Letters of Credence of Swedish envoys before they travel abroad (suit).

And the king is the chairman of the foreign affairs committee, the parliament's ear on the government where members are informed about important foreign policy developments. In this function the king chairs the meetings and calls the speakers but may not ask questions or take part in the discussions, which sometimes become quite heated.

Many previous and current committee

The king has to see all sorts. Here King Carl Gustaf and Queen Margrethe are looking in
on some bovine surgery at the Veterinary High School in Copenhagen.
PHOTO: BERT OLSSON 1975

members tell us that the king handles these meetings faultlessly. He can certainly become a little perplexed when Conservatives and Social democrats are going at each other (about u-boats for instance) but then smoothes it over with his careful summary and a "Fine, so now we can proceed to the next item on the agenda."

Members of the foreign affairs committee are required to "show caution" with the information they get from the committee. When especially sensitive subjects are under discussion it is the king who has the task of deciding whether to make the matter "Top Secret". If the king behaves correctly at these meetings then he can re-

Royal boredom? No, the Swedish king Carl Gustaf and the Danish Queen Margrethe are listening hard but hearing nothing in the sound-proof room at Denmark's Technical High School.
PHOTO: TORBJÖRN ANDERSSON 1975

quire that others behave likewise. For instance, he could not hide his irritation in an incident involving the Socialist Party leader Gudrun Schyman's bleeper.

Mrs Schyman's bleeper went off all of a sudden in the middle of the meeting, not once but twice. It was her teenage daughter Anna who wanted her mother. Gudrun Schyman got up to go out, but the king interrupted to ask what she was doing.

– Phoning my daughter.

– We are not in the habit of doing that here, the king said sternly as Gudrun Schyman slunk back into her chair.

Then it rang again and the king's eyes went as black as thunder. It was headlines next day! Foreign affairs committee members not always being "cautious" with their information.

Ordinary citizens associate the king's official appearances with state visits, the Nobel prizes and the state opening of parliament, when the king holds his traditional address to members of parliament and the Swedish people.

On average the king makes 150 speeches a year, although only three come up every year: in parliament, on radio to expatriate Swedes on Christmas Day and on 6 June for Sweden's

National Day. Particular care is taken in preparing these three speeches.

For several years comments have been made about the increasing length of the royal address at the opening of parliament. Formalists and the king's opponents see intrigues and plots as the king attempts to regain his power. And the king's speech certainly HAS got longer.

When the king opened parliament for the first time in 1975 the address was five lines. Ten years later in 1985 it had lengthened to 19 lines, in 1987/88 it was 32 lines and according to the minutes from the 1995/96 opening of parliament by then it was up to 67 lines!

– As far as I know, the Palace is behind the progressive lengthening of the king's speech at the opening of parliament and it is the Palace that has given it a more politicial and controversial direction, wrote Hans Lindblad, an ex-leader of the Liberal Party (Folkpartiet) in a parliamentary motion.

– The king's address is NOT controversial, but it has substance. He takes up sensitive and important matters but only so as to emphasise that the task for parliament is to tackle these vital issues, the Palace retorts.

Perhaps there are many who believe the king and the Palace alone are responsible for the annual address to parliament. But the prime minister, the speaker of the house and quite a few members of parliament and experts review and edit early drafts before the king presents the final version to parliament.

Before the Christmas Day message to expatriate Swedes, the king is quite prepared to take help from outside speechwriters whom he trusts. One year he was helped for example by the speaker Ingegerd Troedsson, another year by the environmentalist Anders Wijkman.

On Swedish National Day the royal family appears at the traditional ceremony at Skansen in Stockholm. But earlier in the day the king normally travels to some other Swedish town to

Olafur Sigurdsson, Vice Managing Director of Kockums showing the king round the gigantic ship building yard.
PHOTO: BERT OLSSON 1975

make a speech. In palace circles thought is being given at present to starting up a new tradition: to create a Swedish National Day Address that has something important in it for the whole nation. On the 1995 National Day when the king visited Norrköping for example he took up the subject of increasing violence and drug and alcohol abuse.

State visits, inaugurations, jubilees, symposia, gala performances and regional visits – how does the king fit it all in? And with his family and private life as well?

The pressure on the king to involve himself in different causes and events has increased enormously in recent years with the Palace dealing with between 25 and 40 new proposals each week. Can he unveil our monument? Inaugurate the new shopping arcade? Attend our scientific convention? Take part in our concert for peace? And so on.

Previously, when Queen Silvia was 'new', she headed the Palace letter and invitation league, but now the king and the crown princess have moved well ahead of her.

Currently the Palace is economical with the king, both to save his time and to ensure that any cause or event involving the king has just the degree of pomp and ceremonial theatre the hosts are looking for.

The king and the royal family must not fritter away their time on little things. Out with 10-year anniversaries and opening of new industrial areas or hospital wards! 50th anniversary at least, and preferably a centennial! And if it's a complete big new factory or a completely new hospital being opened, then the king may come.

Even if the king never puts his own interests first nonetheless it is obviously easier to get him to show up for something of particular interest to him. If the councillors of Tyresö want the king to open their new national park Tyresta then obviously they should use their trump card, the king's interest in nature.

And if Unicef invites him to a concert where the proceeds go to Brazilian street children then at least the queen will accept and may try that little bit harder to persuade the king to go too. But send out your invitation well ahead of time, preferably two or three years! And avoid Friday evenings if you can as the king is very protective of his weekends with the family.

– Right let's get on with today's meeting. According to the constitution the king chairs the foreign affairs committee where he leads the meetings but may not contribute and the advisory councils where cabinet ministers inform the king about current political matters. The Prime Minister Carl Bildt is waiting to speak.
PHOTO: URBAN BRÅDHE 1991

The Marshal of The Court (Hovmarskalken) or First Marshal to give him his full title, is reponsible for the royal couple's official programme (invitations, inaugurations etc.), state visits and travel.

The Chief of Staff (Stabschefen) is not actually part of the Palace but head of His Majesty's Royal Staff and a part of Sweden's Armed Forces. The Royal Staff consists of 40 men, aides, senior aides and ex-aides. One task of the Chief of Staff is to keep the king briefed on the situation in the armed forces.

The Marshal of The Realm (Riksmarskalken) is the king's right-hand man, responsible for coordinating between palace staff and maintaining regular contact with the government and the parliament.

In the autumn of 1995, for instance, the Swedish company Stora invited the king to the 195th anniversary of their club (Stora Sällskapet) and scheduled for a Friday evening.

– No, but if it it possible to move it to Monday evening then I would be pleased to come replied the king. The dinner was moved and everybody was pleased.

The Palace has begun to manage the king's programme more tightly. Before broadly speaking invitations were accepted from those received. Now the Palace is trying to take the initiative and direct the king's activity a little more, contacting provincial governors, for instance, and asking them for suggestions on what the royal couple might visit around the country.

The Palace and the royal couple plan the official programme together. But the king has two lives of his own outside of his official palace schedule.

Partly there is his private life, which the king looks after himself (Joppe's 50th birthday, sailing with the Philipsons etc.) merely crosschecking with the official schedule. The Palace claims not to know anything about this life although Palace aides are often present.

Partly there are the king's semi-official engagements. These include his presidency of the Worldwide Fund for Nature and of the World Scout Foundation. And these include his traditional trips with the Engineering Science Academy's Royal Technology missions which take the king on study visits all over the world. Most recently he was in South Africa.

Learned lectures, long-winded local councillors, endless government papers, soporific choral singing, the never-ending folk dance teams and gymnastic displays...

Doesn't the king ever fall asleep? I slept like a log when the friends of the Swedish National Museum had their formal annual meeting with the king as the guest of honour last winter. The programme was interesting, there was a good atmosphere, but it was five

curious prince looking in the periscope at the Submarine exhibition in Stockholm...
PHOTO: SYDSVENSKAN 1955

, and an interested king looking in the microscope during a visit to the research insti-
te Idéon, Lund. *PHOTO: PER LINDSTRÖM 1986*

The King's Marshals of the Court:

Tom Wachtmeister 1973–75
Björn von der Esch 1975–1980
Lennart Ahrén 1980–87
Jan Kuylenstierna 1987–93
Hans Ewerlöf 1993–

Brisk breeze around the Lund Cathedral School for its 900th anniversary. Two queens and a king on their way into the cathedral. The Danish Queen was there because the school was Danish until 1658.
PHOTO: PER LINDSTRÖM 1985

One way to celebrate the Cathedral School's anniversary:
a portrait of the royal couple in a shoe shop.
PHOTO: PER LINDSTRÖM 1985

The Danish Queen
Margrethe waving happily
to the people of Lund at
the anniversay of their
Cathedral School and
being applauded by the
Swedish royal couple and
Malmö's provincial gover-
nor couple Ingegerd and
Bertil Göransson.
*PHOTO: PER
LINDSTRÖM 1985*

Thanks for your help. Leif "Loket" Olsson handing over a
cheque for 15 million kronor to the king, president of the
Worldwide Fund for Nature.
PHOTO: JONAS EKSTRÖMER 1995

o'clock in the afternoon; nobody had got round to eating dinner and many had come rushing from a hectic day at work. Fur-
hatted old ladies who had come to look at the king, also nod-
ded off after a little bit of choral singing, one old dear snoring
so loudly that the row in front turned round and hissed at her.

But the king was wide awake! He never falls asleep during official engagements, we are told with reference to his famed
iron condition. Apart from the propellor incident we have
found only one other crack in the royal facade: he doodles!

At weekly palace planning sessions the king sits and scrib-
bles on his agenda, systematically and methodically. Queen Silvia is very careful to throw these royal doodles in the waste paper basket after the meetings. They are not to be saved for an
unsuspecting posterity.

Wet with snow the king opens the World Ski Championships in Falun. *PHOTO: JAN COLLSIÖÖ 1993*

The official tours of every province and county in Sweden is a royal custom dating back to the Middle Ages called "Eriksgata".

The King's "Eriksgata"

Jämtland, March 1974	*Skaraborg, May 1975*
Uppsala, May 1974	*Östergötland, May 1975*
Västmanland, June 1974	*Jönköping, June 1975*
Göteborg and Bohus, September 1974	*Älvsborg, September 1975*
Värmland, September 1974	*Kronoberg, September 1975*
Malmöhus, May 1975	*Västerbotten, June 1976*

The King and Queen's "Eriksgata"

Gotland, May 1978
Kalmar, October 1978
Norrbotten, August 1980
Södermanland, September 1980
Halland, June 1981
Kopparberg, May 1983
Kristianstad, August/September 1983

Örebro, September 1984
Västernorrland, June 1985
Gävleborg, August 1987
Blekinge, May 1988
Härjedalen, August 1989
Gislaved, Gnosjö, Värnamo, April 1990

– My dear Carl Gustaf...a concerned
Queen Silvia getting involved in the
king's attack of coughing on Swedish
Flag Day at Skansen.
The entire royal family are there with
behind them the Marshal of the Realm
Per Sköld and his wife Anna-Stina and
to their right the then church minister
Inger Davidson (Christian Democrats).

PHOTO: URBAN BRÅDHE 1992

No gondola rides in Venice –
the king refused – but a trip in
a motor launch instead during
the state visit to Italy.
PHOTO: ANDERS HOLMSTRÖM 1991

Many find the king's speeches boring. Here Pope John Paul II seems
thoughtful, pondering perhaps whether to have a word with the
king's speech writers. The king paid a courtesy visit to the Vatican
on his state visit to Italy.

PHOTO: ANDERS HOLMSTRÖM 1991

Who hugs first? The affection seems to be mutual between the Soviet leader Leonid Brezjnev and the Swedish king Carl Gustaf in Moscow on a state visit.
PHOTO: URBAN BRÅDHE 1978

The Yugoslavian President Marshal Josip Tito likes uniforms and pomp but here he seems to have more than enough during the visit of the Swedish royal couple. *PHOTO: PER KAGRELL 1978*

Our Swedish royal couple were never the best of friends with the Romanian Presidential couple Elena and Nicolae Ceausescu when they were here on a state visit.

The nature loving Carl Gustaf found Elena's ocelot fur coat a little hard to take with the ocelot an endangered species. And Elena demanded to be an honorary doctor at Uppsala which all authorities ruled was out of the question. After the fall of the presidential couple in 1989 worse scandals came to light but nobody knew anything about them when this picture was taken in the inner courtyard of the Royal Palace in Stockholm.

PHOTO: KENT ÖSTLUND 1980

PLO Leader Yassir Arafat is one of many big international names to have been the guest of King Carl Gustaf at the palace.
PHOTO: GUNNAR SEIJBOLD 1993

Welcome to The White House! Nancy and Ronald Reagan invited the Swedish royal couple to dinner during their New Sweden Journey to the USA and the atmosphere was excellent. They celebrated the 350th anniversary of the landing of the first Swedish settlers at the mouth of the Delaware River in 1638. *PHOTO: TORBJÖRN CARLSON 1988*

During the autumn of 1995 the Swedish royal couple received state visits
from all three of the Baltic states, Estonia, Latvia and Lithuania. The last in line
was the Lithuanian president Algirdas Brazauskas who came in November
and is here inspecting the Svea Lifeguards in the inner courtyard.
PHOTO: TOBIAS RÖSTLUND 1995

When a new foreign ambassador arrives in Sweden he/she presents her credentials to the king at a ceremonial audience.
The ambassador is taken to the Foreign Office in one of the palace cars.
There awaiting them is the 100-year old "Sjuglasvagn" (Seven Glass Carriage) with its team of four horses, its gold-laced cavalier as a driver and two palace footmen on hand to take the ambassador the short way over Norrbro to the palace.
The king wears his admiral's uniform for the audience while the ambassador wears tails or national costume.
When the king and the ambassador meet nobody else may be present.
The meeting lasts about a quarter of an hour.

Oops! The king nearly slips over as he leaves the Swedish naval vessel to go ashore for his state visit to Latvia. *PHOTO: TOBIAS RÖSTLUND 1992*

A three day state visit with President Mary Robinson in Ireland. Did it rain the whole time on the Emerald Isle? *PHOTO: JACK MIKRUT 1992*

It's a case of taking in the local culture. The king greets in Indian fashion when the Swedish royal couple are guests of the president Shankal Dayal Sharma on their state visit to India.
PHOTO: JAN COLLSIÖÖ 1993

The royal couple are as delighted as every other tourist as they enjoy the splendour of the fairy-tale Taj Mahal during their state visit to India.
PHOTO: LEIF R JANSSON 1993

Foreign state visits

1974
NORWAY *King Olav V*
FINLAND *President Urho Kekkonen*

1975
DENMARK *Queen Margrethe II*
ICELAND *President Dr Kristján Eldjárn*
UNITED KINGDOM *Queen Elizabeth II*

1976
NETHERLANDS *Queen Juliana*

1977
BELGIUM *King Baudouin and Queen Fabiola*

1978
SOVIET UNION *Communist Party Chairman Leonid Brezjnev*
YUGOSLAVIA *President Josip Tito*

1979
WEST GERMANY *President and Mrs Walter Scheel*
AUSTRIA *President and Mrs Rudolf Kirchschläger*

1980
JAPAN *Emperor Hirohito*
FRANCE *President and Mrs Valéry Giscard d'Estaing*

1981
TANZANIA *President Julius Nyerere*

SAUDI ARABIA *King Khaled*
CHINA *Government of China*

1982
MEXICO *President and mrs José López-Portillo*
AUSTRALIA *(King only) Governor-General Sir Zelman Cowen*

1983
SPAIN *King Juan Carlos and Queen Sophia*
FINLAND *President and Mrs Mauno Koivisto*
LUXEMBOURG *Grand Duke Jean and Grand Duchess Joséphine-Charlotte*

1984
BRAZIL *President and Mrs Joao Baptista de Oliveira Figueiredo*

1985
SWITZERLAND *Federal Government*

1986
   PORTUGAL *President and Mrs Mário Soares*
   EGYPT *President and Mrs Hosni Mubarak*

1987
   ICELAND *President Vigdís Finnbogadóttir*

1988
   CANADA *Governor-General Jeanne Sauvé*

1989
   NEW ZEALAND *Governor-General and Mrs Reeves*
   JORDAN *King Hussein and Queen Noor*

1991
   ITALY *President Francesco Cossiga*
   VATICAN *Pope John Paul II*
   HUNGARY *President and Mrs Arpád Göncz*

1992
   IRELAND *President Mary Robinson and Mr Robinson*

   LATVIA *President and Mrs Anatolijs Gorbunovs*
   LITHUANIA *President and Mrs Vytautas Landsbergis*

1993
   GERMANY (official visit) *President and Mrs Richard von Weizsäcker*
   NORWAY *King Harald V and Queen Sonja*
   POLAND (King only) *President Lech Walesa*
   INDIA *President Dr Shankal Dayal Sharma*

1995
   CZECH REPUBLIC *President and Mrs Václav Havel*

1996
   Malaysia *King Yang Di-Pertuan Agong*

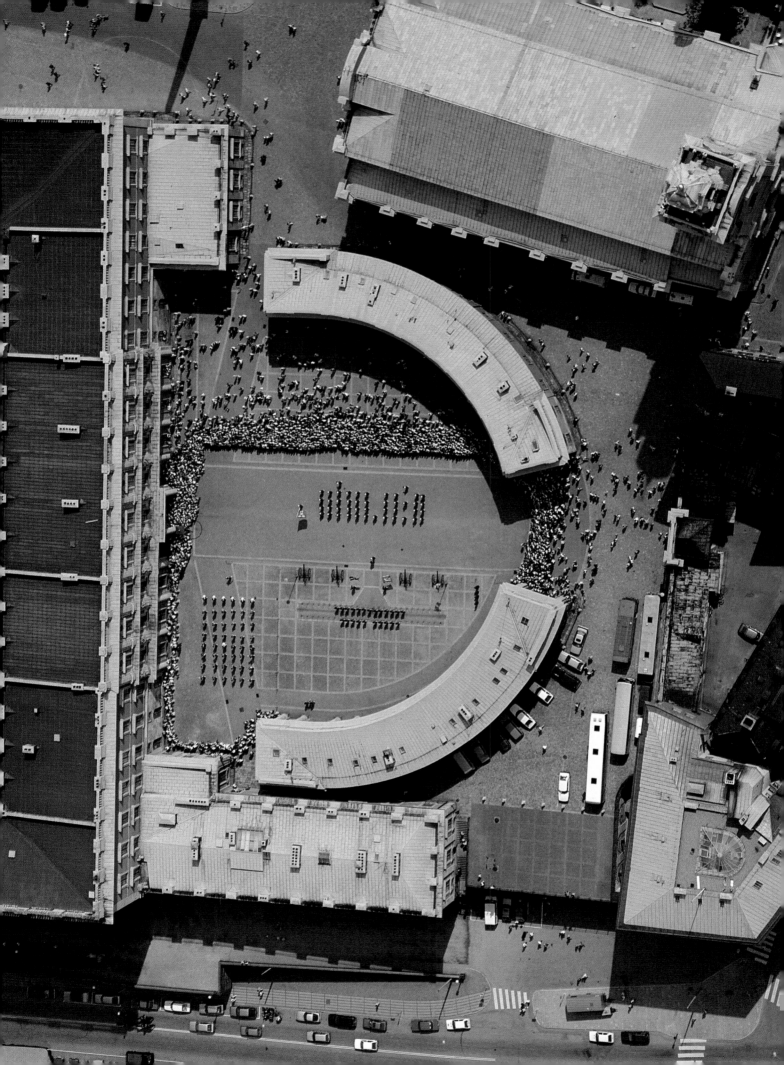

THE KING'S PALACES.

Stockholm Palace

When the Tre Kronor (Three Crowns) Castle of the Vasas burned down in 1697 the palace architect Nicodemus Tessin The Younger had already begun building a new palace facing Norrbro, as the Tre Kronor was out of date and living quarters were cramped. Tessin probably rubbed his hands in glee when Tre Kronor went up in flames because now he could create his baroque masterpiece. But construction was halted in 1707 when the court treasury ran out of money. Karl XII needed money for his wars so palace building had to wait until 1728. Now Carl Hårleman and C.G.Tessin took over and completed the palace in the modern French rococo style.

The Royal Palace in Stockholm was ready by 1754 but had fallen into disrepair by the nineteenth century when Karl XIV Johan complained of having to welcome foreign emissaries in run-down state rooms.

Since then Stockholm Palace has been under continuous renovation. The building is unique because of its blend of Italian baroque, French classicism and rococo. Not even Rome has such a fine example of a baroque building.

Stockholm Palace has 650 furnished rooms and 1200 different rooms in total from the log cellar to the "Vita Havet" (White Sea). Nowadays apart from the state halls and state apartments it functions as the royal couple's place of work – a modern office with top-of-the range computers and 250 palace employees, the palace chapel, the Bernadotte Library, the Great Hall, Treasury, Armoury and Gustav III's museum of antiquities.

It is a living palace in more ways than one. During the 50s and 60s for example the palace began to subside and it was necessary to drill into the granite rocks beneath to underpin the palace foundations and prevent a catastrophe. At present the dirt and grime is being removed from the outside walls of the palace, an operation that will take several years.

Haga Palace

Gustav III dreamed of the palace at Haga as a little Versailles and the most beautiful place on earth. In his grand plans he envisaged a broad mall along the whole length of what is now Sveavägen, linking the Haga Palace with the Royal Palace in Stockholm.
The architect Louis Jean Desprez designed Haga Palace in the New Antique style and work began in 1786. With the death of Gustav III, work stopped but not before the Konungens Paviljong (King's Pavilion) and the Koppartälten (Copper Marquee) had been completed.

An air photograph of the Royal Palace with the king receiving citizens congratulating him on his birthday
PHOTO: TORBJÖRN ANDERSSON 1990

136

The Royal Palace surrounded by The National Museum, The Grand Church (Storkyrkan), and the House of the Nobility.
PHOTO: TORBJÖRN ANDERSSON 1990

The Table That Escaped The King

The king sighed. It was the Haupt table. In the autumn of 1995 the king sat reading the Sotheby's catalogue for the forthcoming sale of the Baron of Baden's collection.

One of the pictures was of this small, elegant and unique tea table made by the world famous Swedish cabinet maker Georg Haupt for Gustav III.

The connoisseur Gustav III had placed the table in the master bedroom at Drottningholm. It stood there for several years until given away by his son Gustav IV Adolf to his mother-in-law Baroness Amalia of Baden in 1804 and it disappeared from Sweden.

That autumn the table was being offered at a price of 200 000–300 000 deutschmarks, about 1.35 million Swedish kronor. The original lower tray had been replaced so large international museums would not be bidding. They only invest in perfect pieces.

The king made a fervent prayer, longing to see the table back in its original place

SOTHEBY´S 1995

in the master bedroom at Drottningholm and on display to the general public.

With the agreement of the royal household, the king decided to bid for the table and agreed a ceiling, an extremely high one considering the royal family's much debated limited allowance.

Royal excitement and expectation were high as bidding started in Baden for the Haupt table. Eventually just two anonymous bidders remained, the Swedish king and a very rich Englishman. The Englishman might have let the Swedish king have the table if he had known who the other bidder was.

But the table went to the Englishman. The king wanted it desperately but he had to withdraw when bidding reached his ceiling at the astronomic sum of 1 495 000 deutschmarks, 7.5 million Swedish kronor with commissions.

Just think, if Peter Wallenberg had known, he could have stepped in and bought the table for the king as a 50th birthday present. After all Queen Silvia got a seven million kronor swimming pool for her 50th birthday.

Under Gustav IV Adolf the C.C.Gjörwell Ekopaviljong and the Queen's Pavilion were added and were then lived in by Karl XIII and Oskar I before being completed in 1932 for the newly married Prince Gustav Adolf and Princess Sibylla. Our present king was born in Haga Palace in 1946 and before that all four Haga princesses had run around and played on the green lawns at Haga.

Haga Palace stood empty throughout the 50s, but in 1964 the Soviet leader Kruschev visited Sweden. Haga Palace, situated on a lake in extensive parkland, was ideal guest accommodation for such government visits, particularly from the security point of view.

In 1966 the royal family agreed to renounce their rights to use the palace and so Haga Palace became a guest hotel for government use.

Since then many prominent guests of the government have stayed there during their visits to Sweden: Aleksey Kosygin (1968), Indira Gandhi (1972), Robert Mugabe (1981), Javier Pérez de Cuéllar (1983), George Bush (1983), Julius Nyerere (1985), Erich Honecker (1986), Yassir Arafat (1988) and others.

Solliden

Queen Victoria had bronchial trouble and wanted to find a summer place with a healthy climate. She chose the Parish of Räpplinge on Öland and had the architect of Stockholm's Olympic Stadium, Torben Grut, design Sol-

Solliden. *SYDSVENSKAN 1950*

liden for her in the Italian style. She paid for it herself.

Solliden was built between 1903 and 1906 and after it was finished Queen Victoria spent every summer there until her death in 1930. She was an austere lady who would wander through the meadows in her self-designed Öland folk costume. When she died she bequeathed her beloved Solliden to her husband Gustav V.

During Gustav V's reign the Haga family were always welcome to spend their summer holidays at Solliden and our current king spent time there nearly every summer. Carl Gustaf inherited Solliden after Gustav V's death in 1950.

Today Solliden is really the royal family's summer place. The grounds are fantastic and include a formal Italian garden, open English parkland, flower gardens and a closeness to the sea ideal for boat trips. The royal couple are actively involved in the management of Solliden and are anxious for the public to experience the charm of the place.

For several years there has been a royal summer exhibition at Solliden. And the royal couple have permitted a "Solliden" perfume to be sold in the souvenir shop.

Stenhammar

The old 1600's manor house in the Parish of Flen was bequeathed to the Swedish state in 1903 by the chamberlain A R von Kraemer.

Payment of a 1000-kronor lease places the property at the disposal of an heir to the throne with the Duke of Södermanland having first refusal.

So it was Prince Wilhelm, Duke of Södermanland, who moved into Stenhammar. He lived here first with his wife, the Russian Grand Princess Maria Pavlovna and their son Lennart (Mainau), and later with his lifelong companion the French lady Jeanne de Tramcourt.

During the 20s, 30s and 40s Stenhammar was a gathering place for painters, authors and artists. Prince Wilhelm with his interests in literature and art invited Bo Bergman, Pär Lagerkvist, Albert Engström, Alma Söderhjelm, Einar Nerman, Karl Ragnar Gierow, Erik Lindorm and many other personalities from the world of culture and the arts to Stenhammar.

When Prince Wilhelm died in 1965 Stenhammar was inherited by Carl Gustaf, who lived at Stenhammar quite often in the beginning taking an active part in managing the farming and forestry on the estate. The total area of the estate is 21 000 hectares and there are five other smaller estates that are leaseholders of the Stenhammar estate. Today the king rarely finds the time to visit Stenhammar. But farming and forestry continues.

Tullgarn Palace

Tullgarn Palace on the Lake Gålö outside Trosa dates from medieval times. In the annals of

The Royal Household at the Royal Palace in Stockholm is responsible for furniture, inventories and works of art in the eight royal palaces and for the upkeep and preservation of the contents of the palaces. The textile collection is one of the foremost in Europe and the furniture collection by the famous cabinet maker Georg Haupt is the largest in Sweden.

A Christmas photograph in the Bernadotte Library at the Royal Palace in Stockholm. *PHOTO: JAN COLLSIÖÖ 1995.*

In the Bernadotte Library at the Royal Palace in Stockholm there are 80 000 books, many magnificently bound. There is also a remarkable collection of photographs, half a million unique pictures all with royal associations. Gustav VI Adolf organised the book collection by the books' owners so in the Bernadotte Library can be found each king's own books, both those received as gifts and those acquired and read by each king. A gold mine for researchers delving into the personality and interests of Swedish royalty.

history they tell of Count Carl Sture's times in the 1580s and of Gustav III's youngest brother Duke Frederik Adolf who transformed Tullgarn into a palace of royal recreation in 1772.

His sister Sofia Albertina was the next to live here. And in 1829 Crown Prince Oskar, later King Oskar I, took over.

It was in the time of King Gustav V and his Queen Victoria that Tullgarn experienced its last period of glory. The royal couple adopted the palace as their summer residence and Gustav V used to go on fishing trips in the bays outside the palace. In the summer of 1909 the entire Russian Tsarist family came to Tullgarn to enjoy some time with the Swedish royal family.

The little prince Carl Gustaf would often visit his great grandfather at Tullgarn when he was young. Today he has the use of the palace and comes here for hunting. In the old inn next to the palace there is a restaurant open to the public in the summer.

Ulriksdal Palace

General and Marshal of the Realm Jacob De la Gardie built Jacobsdal Palace on the western shore of Edsviken outside Stockholm in the 1600s. Hedvig Eleonora later purchased Jacobsdal, renamed it Ulriksdal and gave it as a christening present to her grandson Prince Ulrik who died while still a child.

In 1717 the palace was taken over by the crown for Ulrika Eleonora. Both Adolf Frederik and Gustav III lived at Ulriksdal but in 1822 it was turned into a royal hospital, ie. an old age home for war veterans.

Karl XV had the palace renovated when he lived there and wanted to make Ulriksdal a museum for Swedish and European art. But it never happened.

In 1923 the crown prince Gustav Adolf moved into Ulriksdal with his wife Louise and had one of the rooms furnished with modern Carl Malmsten furniture. Since the death of Gustav VI Adolf, Ulriksdal has effectively been empty. There is a museum and since 1982 one wing has been rented out to the Swedish section of the Worldwide Fund for Nature. Princess

Slussen (The Sluice), Gamla Stan (The Old Town) and crowning it all the Royal Palace in Stockholm.
PHOTO: TORBJÖRN ANDERSSON 1990

141

Christina and her family live in Villa Beylon a stone's throw away from Ulriksdal Palace and the newly renovated theatre Confidencen.

Strömsholm

The Carolinian palace Strömsholm a few Swedish miles outside Västerås was given as a present by Karl X Gustav to Queen Hedvig Eleonora. The palace was ready by 1672, but it was 100 years later that Nicodemus Tessin The Elder's creation was furnished by C F Adelcrantz.

Not many royals have lived at Strömsholm. King Carl Gustaf's father Gustav Adolf did his army riding school training here in his youth and today's royal family is always happy to visit Strömsholm for the annual horse riding events.

In recent times Strömsholm has come to be associated with riding and equestrian sports but there have been horses here for many centuries. The stable buildings have been used for stud farms and as the army's riding school. Today they accommodate a high school for the country's riding instructors.

High season at Strömsholm is in early summer when the big horse race, the Swedish Grand National and the Swedish Showjumping and Dressage Championships take place here bringing with them some 15 000 visitors for "Sweden's largest picnic".

Rosersberg Palace

Rosersberg Palace lies half-way between Stockholm and Uppsala. It was built between 1634 and 1638 and had its heyday in the 19th century.

Karl XIII, the brother of Gustav III, lived at Rosersberg for 50 years in all. Afterwards King Karl XIV Johan and Queen Desideria moved to Rosersberg which later became Desideria's widow seat until her death in 1860.

The military took over the palace in 1876 and currently lease it out for civil defence.

The royal apartments, furnished in Rosersberg's heyday in the 19th century, remain completely intact today.

Gripsholm Castle

Gripsholm Castle outside Mariefred about fifty miles from Stockholm was built at the end of the 14th century by Bo Jonsson Grip and was named after his coat of arms. Albrekt of Mecklenburg swore his oath of allegiance here.
Sten Sture bought the castle in the 15th century and gave it to the monks so that for a time Gripsholm was a monastery.

Gripsholm was really a fortress and was very uncomfortable to live in. But Gustav Vasa, his three queens one after the other and his sons lived in the castle at various times. Johan III and his family were imprisoned here for four years on the orders of his brother Erik XIV. And Erik himself was held captive here as was later Gustav IV Adolf.

Over the centuries the 450-year old castle has been lived in by various kings, but especially by their widowed queens. Gustav III had apartments prepared in the castle for his family and rebuilt the theatre.

Up until the 19th century Gripsholm was lived in by the royal family, but is now a museum housing Sweden's portrait collection that includes some 4000 portraits of famous Swedes up to the modern day.

Drottningholm Palace

In 1981 the royal family left the exhaust fumes and traffic noise of the royal palace in Stockholm and moved out to the beautifully situated and much more child-friendly Drottningholm a few miles west of Stockholm.

It is the queens who have left their mark on Drottningholm over the centuries. Johan III, Gustav Vasa's son, built the first palace at the end of the 16th century for his queen Katarina Jagellonica naming it Drottningholm after her.

Gripsholm Castle on Lake Mälaren with Mariefred in the background. *PHOTO: TORBJÖRN ANDERSSON 1990.*

The palace burnt down in 1661 and was rebuilt by the widowed queen Hedvig Eleonora. The famous palace architect Nicodemus Tessin The Elder designed and planned the palace which was completed after his death by his son Nicodemus Tessin The Younger.

One of the queens at Drottningholm was Lovisa Ulrika who received the palace as a wedding gift when in 1744 she married the heir to the throne Adolf Fredrik. Her son Gustav III took over Drottningholm and is really the one who made the palace famous. More recent kings and queens have also lived at Drottningholm, Oskar I for example and Joséphine, Gustav V and Victoria as well as Gustav VI Adolf and Louise.

Nowadays it is the turn of the current royal family to enjoy the beautiful surroundings, the symmetrically constructed baroque garden, the romantic English parkland and the waters of Lake Mälaren that surround Drottningholm Palace where at least Prince Wilhelm in his time claims to have stumbled upon a real palace ghost.

Drottningholm Palace in winter attire.
PHOTO: TORBJÖRN ANDERSSON 1990

— One Needs a Little Luck in Life.

There are times when the king feels the need to get away. To leave his official duties behind and withdraw into the country, onto the fells or out to sea. But only in his own time. Then into the car or boat go the family and his aide and off they go with the king at the wheel, and preferably at night.

Gotska Sandön is one of the places he likes. The entire royal family comes here nearly every summer aboard the motor cruiser Ancylus which provides rocking accommodation for them when they get there. When the children were younger they loved playing on the long stretches of sandy beaches free from photographers and bystanders.

With the family asleep in their bunks the king has sometimes taken the dinghy and rowed into the island where he would sit enjoying the solitude, the peace and serenity of the island as the sea lapped on the unspoilt beaches. He was sitting like this one day when a group of tourists strolled by. The king? Here? Taken aback for a moment, but recovering quickly, they timidly asked if they could take a picture.

Firmly the king said no. He wanted to be alone. And he asked them to respect the fact that at times he wanted to be left in peace. There were no pictures.

The king has a special affinity with nature. It has a relaxing influence on him.

The whispering of the pine trees, the beauty of the flowering meadows and the melancholy of the lakes awake the same emotions in the king as in every Swede who has ever held the dream of a plot of their own in their hearts. And the demands of the king's stiff ceremonial life provide twice as much reason for escaping and being one with nature, free from official constraint.

One remarkable experience that made a deep impression on the king was the time he accompanied the wild life photographer Bertil Pettersson to watch at a bear hide in the forest outside Strömsund.

They stayed on watch for two evenings and nights and from their hide they saw elks, black grouse and other animals. Then quite suddenly in the dim light of dusk a bear came lumbering towards them.

But not just one. To the king's undisguised delight another bear came along. In front of the king's camera and captured on video the two bears came together and honoured the king with one of the great dramas of the wild, one almost too awesome to take in. Afterwards talking to Expressen, the king could only say:

– One needs a little luck in life!

The king's interest in the environment, in nature and in the natural sciences is well documented, so it is hardly a coincidence to find that he is president of the Swedish committee of the Worldwide Fund for Nature, the World Scout Foundation and the Royal

Alone at last! Nobody would begrudge the royal couple this: to escape the fuss and the protocol, to be alone experiencing together the grandeur of nature, enjoying the rhythms of a healthy body, or delighting in the relaxation of tired minds and muscles. *PHOTO: JAN COLLSIÖÖ 1993*

Swedish Council for the Protection of Countryside and Heritage, and takes part each year in a "Royal Technology Mission", the natural sciences travel programme arranged by the Academy of Engineering Science.

The king has supported the Worldwide Fund for Nature since its inception in 1971. Initially he was honorary president, but in 1986 he took on the job of chairman. The Worldwide Fund for Nature's Swedish board of trustees meets twice a year and Carl Gustaf has not missed a single meeting in 25 years.

It says something about the king's interest, says Jens Wahlstedt, previously head of the Worldwide Fund for Nature. And

when complimenting him on attending all the meetings, his usual reply is to say modestly that it is nothing remarkable. "You ask me first when I can make it and arrange the meeting accordingly."

If the king is a door opener for Swedish business abroad, his contribution is no less for environmental projects both here at home and overseas.

A brother to the queen was getting married in Brazil so Jens Wahlstedt and Jonas Wahlström from Skansen approached the king and briefed him about the endangered lion monkey. Their only known habitat was in Brazil, in a reserve outside

But this is reality. Photographer Jan Collsiöö managed to take the beautiful picture of the royal couple making their way in solitude towards Treriksröset along the newly opened 500-mile Nordic Way. But behind them comes this enormous entourage which includes Norwegian King Harald and Queen Sonja, aides, bodyguards, media and all the rest.
PHOTO: JAN COLLSIÖÖ 1993

As a child Carl Gustaf loved to do things, always fixing, pottering and whittling and generally working with his hands. He has a practical bent and his children and his sisters' children will bear witness to the fact that he always – almost – succeeds in mending their broken toys. Here he is clearing the forest at Solliden. If Carl Gustaf had not been born a king he could certainly have become "something in farming or forestry". *PHOTO: CLAS GÖRAN CARLSSON 1972*

Rio, and this was in danger of being wiped out by a dam construction project. Could the king help save the lion monkey on his Brazilian trip, Wahlstedt and Wahlström wondered.

The king explained that he could not influence foreign ministers directly but he could and would ask questions about the project.

And this he did. The Brazilian ministers were surprised by the Swedish king's knowledge and interest and soon pulled a few strings. The dam site was shifted and the lion monkeys are now in the best of health and increasing in numbers.

The king has also taken an active part in the project to save the Indian tiger from extinction.

But he is just as likely to be found in his own free time without any entourage visiting Lake Tåkern bird sanctuary and seeing for himself how the bird population stands and how the various improvements are coming

The king and master of the royal hunt Lambert von Essen are well-equipped to confront their prey at an annual royal invitation hunt on the Halleberg and Hunneberg plateaux in Västergötland. *PHOTO: BERTIL PETTERSSON 1978*

along. It was here he took his three children to watch the geese.

In the autumn of 1995 the king went to Germany to take a long hard look at the restoration of the environmentally damaged Ruhr Valley. Shortly afterwards the trustees of the Worldwide Fund for Nature were delighted to find themselves listening to a full off-the-cuff report of his findings.

– Straight from the heart, knowledgeable, well-informed and incredibly interesting. I just wished every Swede could have

heard the king. So different from his official speeches, commented one fortunate witness.

In the Royal Swedish Council for the Protection of Countryside and Heritage, other members are impressed by the king's knowledge of Djurgården and Ulriksdal.

– He knows the lie of every hill, he knows the roads, the trails and the slopes. And he has a "green" attitude to incursions into the environment seeking always to avoid encroachment into the land and countryside.

152

Peace, the future, visions. The king has to support them all, but when the cause concerns the natural world or the environmental then he is more than happy to do so. Here he opens the unique Eco park, Stockholm by symbolically releasing a dove of peace.

PHOTO: BJÖRN LARSSON ASK 1995

When something interests him King Carl Gustaf is not so different from his grandfather
Gustav VI Adolf excited by some archaeological find. What the king is studying so intensely
in the water tank are the 50 000 crayfish he will be releasing into Riddarfjärden shortly.
PICA PRESSFOTO 1993

He has an intimate knowledge of the royal
historic palaces, particularly the Royal Palace in Stockholm. He is not as well versed with
some of the others but he always takes an interest in discussions about them, witness
members of the king's council, to give it its
day-to-day name.

The king's love of nature takes many
forms, as the media are quick to remind us:
skiing vacations at Storlien, boat trips with
Ancylus, helicopter flights in the Alps, reindeer round-ups in Lapland, flower cultiva-
ting in Solliden, trekking in the Swedish fells
or in Bhutan, deep sea diving, scouting and
survival courses. And hunting! Ask any of the
197 members of the Royal Hunt and you will

For 48 tense hours the king sat watching in the Jämtland forest hoping to see a bear...
PHOTO: BERTIL PETTERSSON 1984

hear what an interested, prudent and discerning hunter the king is, shooting as well with a rifle as with a shotgun.

Each year the king hosts two "Royal Invitation Hunts". One takes place in Bergslagen when twenty hand-picked friends and leading businessmen are invited to hunt elk and then dine and overnight at Färna manor house. Last time Anders Wall, Gustaf Douglas, Peter Forssman, Marcus Wallenberg jr and Carl Johan Bonnier were among those invited.

The other royal invitation hunt takes place on the Halleberg and Hunneberg plateaux in Västergötland and have a more international flavour. Here heads of state and foreign royalty mix with hunters from the upper strata of Swedish society with overnighting at Koberg, the house of the king's brother-in-law Niclas Silfverschiöld.

– The king is an exemplary hunter and a first class hunt host. He would never dream of taking up the best positions himself for instance, commented one impressed fellow

...coming lumbering alon

ddenly this enormous bear showed up, and then another, and the king's life is enriched by the glorious memory.

PHOTO: BERTIL PETTERSSON 1984

Vega Hat. *PHOTO: LEIF R JANSSON 1980*

Military Hat Model 59. *PHOTO: PER LINDSTRÖM 1975*

Chef's Hat. *PHOTO: ANDERS HOLMSTRÖM 1986*

Hats fit for a king.

Queen Silvia always wears elegant hats on official occasions and these are the subject of endless comments and innumerable pictures. But at least she can choose them herself.

The king acquires all sorts of weird and wonderful head gear in the course of his official and private life, but rarely does he have much say in the choosing. If it is not some safety helmet or military cap being forced upon him, then it is folk costume attire from a foreign country.

Here is a small selection of all the helmets, turbans, caps and much else the king has been pictured wearing over the years at home and abroad.

Now it is the king's turn to have a hat parade!

Engine Driver's Cap.
PHOTO: JAN FORSMAN 1978

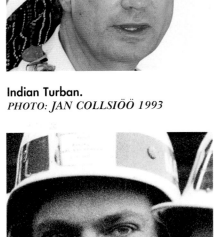

Indian Turban.
PHOTO: JAN COLLSIÖÖ 1993

Miner's Helmet.
PHOTO: LEIF R JANSSON 1973

Wolf Cub Cap.
PHOTO: R FERNEBORG 1957

Fireman's Helmet.
PHOTO: TORBJÖRN CARLSON 1977

Doctor's Hat
PHOTO: KENT HULT 1985

Sombrero.
PICA PRESSFOTO 1952

Bilberry Pixie Hat.
PHOTO: ANDERS WIKLUND 1994

Jewish Skullcap.
PHOTO: RAGNHILD HAARSTAD 1975

Protective "Boat" Hat.
SCANDIA PHOTOPRESS 1975

Uniform Cap.
PHOTO: PER LINDSTRÖM 1982

Hunting Hat.
PHOTO: URBAN BRÅDHE 1992

Student Cap.
SVENSKT PRESSFOTO 1966

Mexican Hat.
PHOTO: LARS NYBERG 1982

Sports Hat.
PHOTO: LARS PORNE 1993

Uniform Cap.
PHOTO: JAN COLLSIÖÖ 1981

Snow Scooter Helmet.
PHOTO: KENNETH PAULSSON 1995

Protective Plastic.
PHOTO: ANDERS HOLMSTRÖM 1984

family

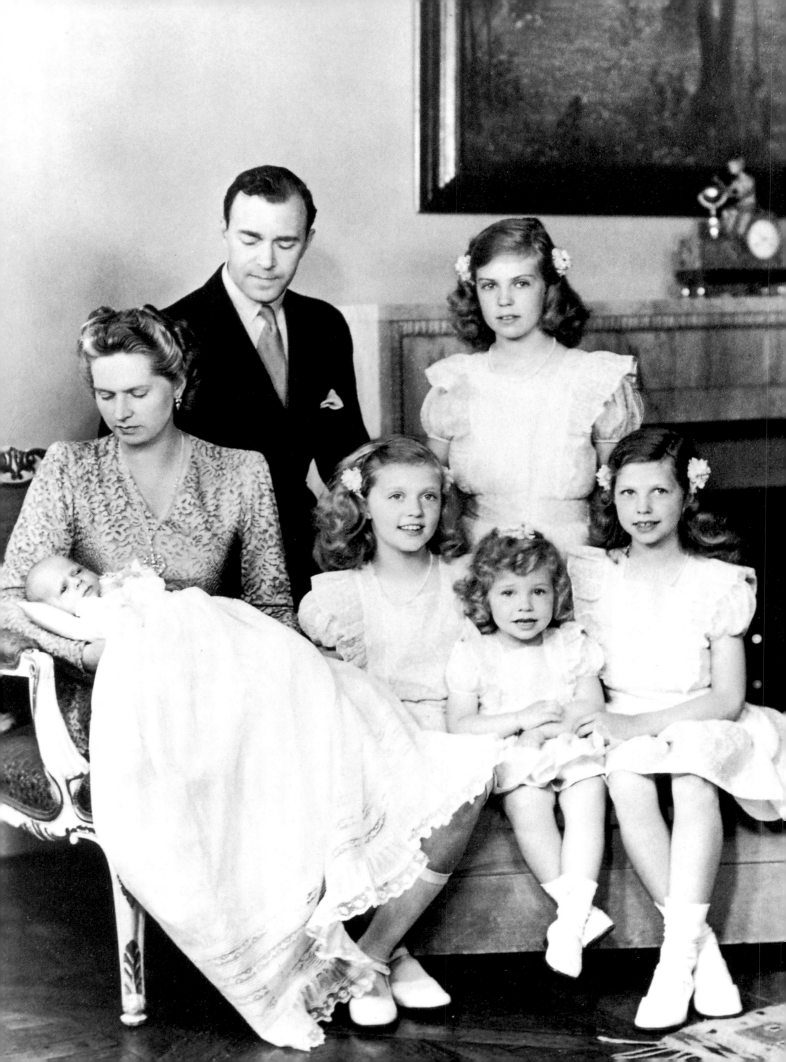

– HE WOULD HAVE MADE A BETTER CABINET-MAKER.

The best decision the king ever made was to propose to Silvia Renate Sommerlath.

The fairy tale wedding between Silvia and Carl Gustaf in the summer of 1976 was followed by the whole world and effectively silenced the debate on introducing a republic to Sweden. With the wise and beautiful Silvia at his side the king acquired a new confidence and maturity. Together they make a very popular and much-admired team that spreads glamour, style and a sense of occasion to domestic events while providing Sweden with much valuable PR abroad. And it is safe to state that the king and queen are popular. Just look at the opinion polls!

In recent years Swedes have made the king top of their list of the most popular living Swedes according to SIFO figures. Before that it was the head of Volvo P G Gyllenhammar who was top. But since the failure of his Renault affair his star has fallen to fifth place and the king has risen from second to first place, a position he has held since 1994.

Queen Silvia lies second in the list of popular living Swedish women behind the unbeatable author Astrid Lindgren. But in the king's heart Silvia is very much number one according to friends who regularly meet the royal couple. They talk about the high regard and admiration the king shows for his wife.

They have a warm intimacy and there is harmony between them, regular eye contact across the dining table and a good "feeling" of closeness.

Little of this is seen in public where the king and queen behave correctly and neutrally towards each other. Many think this is a shame, wanting to see more contact, intimacy and spontaneity between the king and the queen and naming the Danish Queen Margrethe and her husband Henrik as examples of a relaxed royal couple with a sparkling presence.

But when Crown Princess Victoria gave her age of maturity address to parliament last summer – with dash and verve – then not even her well-drilled parents could keep their strict royal facades. Moved, proud, smiling and a little relieved both the king and the queen for once allowed their feelings to show in public in front of the TV cameras.

– The king was of course proud as punch, commented an even prouder Palace official. Those who have lived close to the royal family in different situations are eager to tell of what a fantastic and considerate family father the king is.

He goes in for his father role 100% taking every opportunity to relax with Silvia and the children. But he is also incredibly active with the family, thinking up fun things to do and exciting places to go, taking the family with

A unique picture of the entire Haga family. A few months later the father of the five children Gustav Adolf was torn away from them in a plane crash in Copenhagen. Gustav Adolf was an officer, much interested in sport, horses and riding and an accomplished swordsman. Princess Sibylla came from Germany, had a good liberal arts education and dreamed of becoming an architect before she met the Swedish Prince Gustav Adolf.
BERNADOTTEBIBLIOTEKET 1946

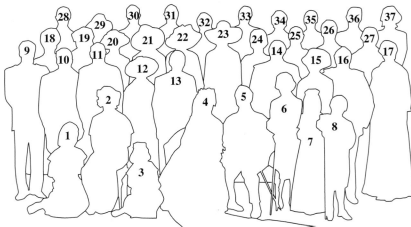

The entire family circle and a few besides, in this classic pict
taken at King Carl Gustaf's and Queen Silvia's wedding.

1. Sophie Sommerlath 2. Carmita Sommerlath
3. Annelie Middelschulte 4. Queen Silvia
5. King Carl Gustaf 6. Prince Hubertus von Hohenzollern
7. Hélène Silfverschiöld 8. James Ambler
9. King Baudouin of Belgium
10. President Kristján Eldjárn, Iceland
11. President Urho Kekkonen, Finland
12. Bride's mother Alice Sommerlath
13. Bride's father Walther Sommerlath 14. Prince Bertil
15. Queen Ingrid, Denmark 16. King Olav, Norway

him on trips, adventures in the country and sporting activities.

Over the years the king has treated his children to barbecues, survival courses and reindeer round-ups in the fells. He has fastened their slalom boots, built them igloos and untangled their fishing lines.

When Victoria was confirmed, her confirmation friends were put up overnight in a barn at Solliden. During the day the king entertained the youngsters with games, boat trips and sports competitions.

During family rambles and nature treks it is always father who remembers to stuff some extra chocolate bars away in his pocket to encourage tired youngsters to keep going. He is quite prepared to carry twice as heavy a pack as anyone else and often ends up carrying the children's rucksacks.

Before each ski trip, whether to their own house in Storlien or to the Alps, the king chases his three children out onto the ski trails on Drottningholm for hard training. He is anxious to make sure they are in good shape for their skiing vacation and will not hear any moaning about aches and pains!

This is of course no more than every decent father does and of course the king has the money and the opportunity. But although this is true, the fact is that he does it all the time with never a break and with an air of matter-of-factness, inventiveness and consideration that leaves most of his fellow parents dumbfounded. He really enjoys it! And the children are well brought up, natural, undemanding and not at all spoilt.

The king often takes his children with him on official engagements if they might get something out of it. Several years ago at the opening of the new Vasa museum the royal couple took Prince Carl Philip and one of Princess Christina's sons with them. For a whole hour the boys sat and endured the inaugural speeches longing for the moment they could go aboard the exciting ship, play with the new computers and have fun. But when the speeches were over, the inaugural committee led the guests quickly around the exhibits and then out through a back entrance. Such was the royal disappointment that the king

167

17. Queen Margrethe, Denmark
18. Queen Fabiola, Belgium 19. Mrs Halldora Eldjárn, Iceland
20. Princess Christina 21. Princess Désirée 22. Princess Birgitta
23. Princess Margaretha 24. Grand Duchess Joséphine Charlotte, Luxembourg 25. Grand Duke Jean, Luxembourg
26. Prince Henrik, Denmark
27. President Walter Scheel, West Germany 28. Walter L Sommerlath 29. Mrs Michele Sommerlath
30. Baron Niclas Silfverschiöld 31. Prince Johann Georg von Hohenzollern 32. Mrs Charlotte Sommerlath
33. Mr John Ambler 34. Mr Tord Magnusson
35. Mr Rolf Sommerlath 36. Mr Jörg Sommerlath
37. Mrs Mildred Scheel

The king's wisest decision was to marry the beautiful Silvia Sommerlath.
The fairy tale wedding in Stockholm was followed by the whole world and started quite a tourist rush to the city.
Do you see how many people had rushed into town on a summer Saturday just to cheer the wedding couple? Silvia's dress in ivory silk was created by Marc Bohan at Dior. The long train was lace-edged and had been worn previously by the Princesses Birgitta and Désirée as had the royal diadem with its cameos and pearls set in red gold.
SYDSVENSKAN 1976

wondered whether they could not look at the Vasa herself.
After a moment's confusion – the Palace had told the committee the royal couple were in a rush to get home and had not planned a visit aboard the ship – a proper tour was arranged for the royal couple and the boys. The boys were even allowed to remain behind and play with the computers.

Last autumn the king invited his family to Germany over the All Saints Day holiday. They visited Dresden, Munich, his mother Sibylla's old family palace Coburg and looked at art and treasures at various museums. The king's brother-in-law Johann Georg, head of the Pinakoteket museum in Munich came along as their guide.

For their 1995 Christmas trip – Kenya – it was Victoria who got to decide. As a reward for being good during the year! Just now the king and queen are pondering over Victoria's future education after her university entrance examination. The king is happy for his daughter to have more time for herself, as she does not need to be rushed through her education in society so quickly as he had to with his grandfather the king approaching ninety.

Victoria will be allowed to study what she wants but must still

It is customary for the press photographers to meet the royal family before the Christmas festivities and take some pleasant pictures. In order to get the children to liven up the photographers normally get some amusing toy for them. For Christmas 1982 it was a musical box which at least six month old Madeleine likes. *PHOTO: KENT HULT 1982*

have a special royal education. She must obviously learn languages properly and the king also wants her to do military service! After all she will be head of the three armed services.

The king obviously has a special relationship with his eldest daughter Victoria because she will succeed him as head of state. But to assume that he therefore makes her his favourite is incorrect. He is actually more anxious about Carl Philip, who is "in the middle" between the heir to the throne Victoria and his little sister Madeleine who everybody makes a fuss of because she is the youngest. The king tries to take Carl Philip out hunting when he can and has described the pleasure he gets when father and son sit together out in the forest watching and waiting.

Many people have wondered why Carl Philip spent so long away in his American school outside New York. The reason is that Carl Philip, like so many other school children, wanted to study abroad, learn the language and perhaps have a change to be a "normal" schoolboy instead of always being in the public eye as would have been the case here at home.

Carl Philip went away after eighth grade. If he had come back already after one year he would have landed in a completely new class for his ninth and last year of school before gym-

Carl Gustaf had to grow up without a father. That may be why he spends so much time with his own children. He is always finding fun things to do and takes them to any official engagements they might enjoy. This time the choice was easy: Kolmården Zoo. *PHOTO: JAN FORSMAN 1993*

nasium. It was better to stay in the USA a year and start direct with new schoolmates in "first ring".

The king is happy to share Madeleine's enormous interest in riding. He does not ride himself, but he is happy to sneak away to the royal stables and get involved in Madeleine's riding lessons.

Perhaps the king throws himself into his father role becasue he did not have the chance to grow up with a father himself. An ideal father?

– One is who one is and that's the way it is. One can try to be close friends to one's children, but one should not set oneself up as some ideal father figure. Anyway there is no such person, the king said in a Sydsvenskan interview a few years ago.

Little has been written about the king's own parents, Prince Gustav Adolf and Princess Sibylla. Gustav Adolf (1906–1947)

Doesn't Carl Gustaf look just like his father Gustav Adolf?
Magazine Se, Number 5 1947.

(1908–1972) as a single parent was alone responsible for her five children's upbringing. She was born in Germany and during the war and the after-war years, it was not easy for her to find a place in the hearts of the Swedish people.

She was never given a chance, it was written after her death. Her relative Estelle Bernadotte, once married to Folke Bernadotte, wrote in an obituary on Sibylla that she had a "strong inner softness but a hard prickly exterior that did most harm to herself". She was not intellectual but she was wise and thoughtful and quick both to tears and laughter.

Sibylla could "give the impression of flightiness and superficiality but when it really mattered she was a staunch character and always a friend to her friends." She was strong and did not show how hard she was finding it.

Sibylla watched over her children's education at a time when the monarchy hung on Olof Palme's famous "stroke of a pen" which

Prince Bertil, Uncle Nappe, has been a big support for Carl Gustaf through the years. Carl Gustaf obviously inherited the motor prince's interest in cars but it was also nice and comforting to hold Uncle Nappe's hand during official galas and events.

SYDSVENSKAN 1954

was an officer, interested in horses and riding, a swordsman and very keen on sport. As chairman in the Swedish Sports Federation he led the Swedish team at the Olympic Games in Berlin in 1936, Hitler's great PR triumph, and greeted Adolf Hitler. Pictures were taken which today lie buried deep in the archives.

Every day the little Haga-sisters helped their father take off his riding boots, Nenne tells us. In return he sang them operatic arias when it was time for bed and got the young girls so excited they became wild and "afterwards it was well-nigh impossible to keep them in any sort of order".

After the 1947 air crash tragedy in which Gustav Adolf was killed, Princess Sibylla

might easily have changed Sweden from a monarchy to a republic. She was not a great believer in an inherited monarchy according to Palace sources and did not really expect her son ever to be king.

A minister of state at that time who once had Princess Sibylla as his companion to the table at a jubilee dinner was greatly surprised when she suddenly explained that she thought her son better suited to being a cabinet-maker than king of Sweden.

It did not turn out at all as Princess Sibylla had expected. The same year she died, her son met Sylvia for the first time.

One year later he became king.

And 20 years further on Sibylla's son was the most admired man in Sweden!

THE KING DOESN'T DIS-OWN THOSE WHO SHOW THEMSELVES UP.

The king has many private friends and a large circle of acquaintances outside the court and his official life. This breaks with the traditions of his predecessors Gustav V and Gustav VI Adolf who only associated with their court and their own relatives.

The king's private friends matter to him, particularly the really old ones from Broms and Sigtuna, and he is regarded as extremely loyal and faithful to his old mates.

They may show themselves up, lose fortunes or become alcoholics – the king will not fail them.

But of course he winces at times. When his really close friend Anders Lettström divorced a few years back and had children with his new wife a little too quickly – not even his closest friends were able to keep up with the sudden change of course – the king was also put out. But he did not turn his back on the friendship.

The question of who exactly is closest to the king and who is in the inner circle is discussed intensely both within the outer circle and in the media. Information changes and asking different friends of the king to list his five closest friends gives many different answers.

There are also so many different circles: old pals from Broms and Sigtuna, the party crowd, family, friends from his hunting and environmental set and so on.

But Anders Lettström is certainly one of those in the king's innermost circle and Jejje Brodin, Björn Kreuger, Magnus Uvnäs, Raoul Hamilton and Erik Lallerstedt and their wives will also be found there.

Anders Lettström is a successful businessman and was previously managing director of Reinhold Property Developments, staying in property even after his bankruptcy. The royal family like to drop in on the Lettströms' at their pleasant home on the Sköldnora royal estate in Upplands Väsby.

Hans Eric "Jejje" Brodin has been a friend since their Broms years, and he and his wife Putzi often accompany the king in his motor boat. At present he sells fire alarms for a living and his wife worked previously for the Beijers auction house in Stockholm.

Björn Kreuger is a lawyer and one of the king's old partying set. His wife Agneta has become a close friend to the queen, as has her daughter Caroline to Victoria.

Magnus Uvnäs belongs to the circle of the king's hunting and environmental friends. He owns the hunting shop Widforss on Fredsgatan in Stockholm and accompanied the royal couple on their Bhutan journey the other year, along with the new mayor of Nynäshamn Anders Byström married to the not

What a catch! The roach the king caught on a fishing trip together with his very best and oldest friends Hans Eric "Jejje" Brodin.
PHOTO: CLAS GÖRAN CARLSSON 1974

altogether unknown singer Lill Lindfors – who had to say no to the trip.

Carl Johan Smith has been around from play school at the Royal Palace to Broms and Sigtuna. He is a bank director with SE-Banken and is married to Annelie who works in a boutique on Humlegårdsgatan in Stockholm.

Also still around from the really old times is Hans-Eric von der Groeben who works nowadays for Handelsbanken in New York. His old crowd also includes Carl Kleman, a chartered economist and Johan Beckman, a financier in London and Paris.

Carl and Christina de Geer at Stora Wäsby Estate north of Stockholm are known for their entertaining theme parties and masquerades. The king loves to dress up and is always happy to show up.

Do you remember the gondola incident in Venice when the king refused to perform for the PR people by jumping down into a waiting gondola in front of the expectant photographers and the world press?

Soon afterwards the royal couple turned up at a de Geers' masquerade carrying a portable toy gondola with the king dressed as a gondolier in striped shirt and braces and the queen playing the part of a tourist.

The pair were an instant hit of course!

Another close friend is the attorney Fred Wennerholm, recently married to Catharina von Baumgarten, daughter of Bokpalatset's Marianne von Baumgarten.

Fred is the son of the old head of Sandrews and attorney Eric Wennerholm and was previously married to Caroline Fleetwood, the department secretary at the foreign office's press agency. Last summer Caroline remarried to the economics professor and managing director of SNS, Hans T:son Söderström.

Other close friends of the royal couple in the legal profession are Ankie and Fredrik Ramberg and Hans Ulrik von der Esch (brother of the Conservative Party politician Björn) and his wife Marianne, school friend of the king from Sigtuna and today busy as

Hunt lunch eaten standing up or sitting on spruce-strewn benches. On this occasion Gad Rausing, Jacob Palmstierna, Erik Penser and Peter Wallenberg are seen out with the royal hunt. *PHOTO: URBAN BRÅDHE 1993*

an attorney at the justice department. Their sons Ulrik and Fredrik von der Esch are part of Victoria's teenage scene.

Businessmen in the king's inner circle of friends: Anders Wall and his wife Charlotte, formerly Palmstierna, Antonia Ax:son Johnson, Peter Wallenberg, Fredrik "Frippe" Palmstierna, Jacob's younger brother and an old Sigtuna pal.

Pehr G Gyllenhammar's star is in decline. It seems his French was a little TOO good when he accompanied the king on his French state visit. It can easily get a little crowded with an emperor and a king.

Someone who would like to be thought of as a close friend of the king is Sven Philip-Sörensen, son of the founder of Securitas. He is happy, generous and "considerate to Lilian". Sörensen is one of the royal couple's wilder friends inviting them on crazy overseas escapades.

2. Krocketklubben (The Royal Swedish Lawn Croquet Club)

3. H.M. Konungens Jaktklubb (The Royal Hunt Club)

The Punsch Club is a leftover from his school days when as teenage lads they would meet to eat pea soup and drink warm Swedish "punsch". It has recently celebrated its 30th anniversary despite signs of increasing tubbiness among some of the young gentleman. Members try to get together once or twice a year.

Just how much croquet is played at the Lawn Croquet Club is open to question. Previously members met every month or so, but with many living abroad and the king's time increasingly precious they no longer see each other quite so often.

It is not easy to find out exactly who belongs to these clubs. Some people seem to be members of two and some of all three. Perhaps it is the belonging that really matters and not the membership card. So we are left with little choice but to bunch all the names up together: the king and honoured members please excuse me. Once a year wives may attend – true at least for the Punsch Club.

SO: Erik Lallerstedt, taverner; Carl-Adam "Noppe" Lewenhaupt, divorced from "Grynet" Molvig and inventive telephone-tending director at Geddesholm outside Västerås; Christer Tegnér, wine agent; Anders Lettström; Carl Johan Smith; Hans Eric von der Groeben; Anders Åhlberg, furniture; Anders Ihre, chartered economist; Johan Åkerhielm, descendant of cork director Wicander (Harpsund) and working for Handelsbanken in Stockholm; Johan Beckman, a London banker; Daniel Bonnier (son of Lukas) and a managing director in the Bonnier Group; Hans-Jacob Bonnier (son of Johan, Jojja) and also a managing director in the Bonnier Group; Peter Degermark, brother of Pia Degermark; Carl Kleman, chartered economist; Fredrik Skiöldebrand, Paris-based entrepreneur; Michael Olenius, plastic surgeon at Karolinska (no he has not given Silvia a facelift!); Björn Åkerlund, Chartered Engineer in the computer business.

And then of course all the wives...

"Lettström dreams them up and Sörensen pays for them", is how the more cynical see matters.

Private political friends are few, really only the provincial governor Ulf Adelsohn and his wife Lena, and Ulf Dinkelspiel whose wife Louise is a teacher at Enskilda High School, where she has taught Crown Princess Victoria.

Friends say that one of the trends of recent years has been for his inventive practical joking set with whacky ideas (and plenty of money!) to throw at the king's limited free time, have kept the royal couple away from their old safe and reliable childhood friends who spend much less time with the king nowadays.

Nonetheless the king likes to stick to his old habits, so he seldom misses meetings of three of his favourite clubs:

1. Punschklubben (The Punsch Club – punsch is a Swedish liqueur)

The Royal Hunt Club plays in a different league. It is not as small as the Punsch and Lawn Croquet clubs, but still fairly exclusive with its 197 members and hundreds of years of custom and tradition. The king holds the presidency for life or "as long as it pleases His Majesty to retain it" and has an important say in the admission of new members.

The Royal Hunt Club's purpose is to promote hunting and preserve game stocks. Each year the club organises a gathering at the Royal Palace to attend a lecture on hunting.

Many members of the Punsch and Lawn Croquet clubs are also members of the Royal Hunt Club.

Other regular members are Peter Wallenberg, Björn Sprängare, Anders "Aje" Philipson, Björn von der Esch, Hans Peder Hagen, Johann Georg von Hohenzollern, Raoul Hamilton, Peter Oleinikoff, Carl Gustaf Klingspor, John Ambler and Johan Nordén.

Foreign State Visits in Sweden

The king as host:

1975
FINLAND *President Urho Kekkonen*
NORWAY *King Olav V*

1976
  YUGOSLAVIA *President Josip Tito*
  AUSTRIA *Federal President and Mrs Rudolf Kirchschläger*

The royal couple as host and hostess:

1979
  SPAIN *King Juan Carlos and Queen Sophia*

1980
  MEXIKO *President and Mrs José López-Portillo*
  ROMANIA *President and Mrs Nicolae Ceausescu*

1981
  CANADA *Governor-General and Mrs Edward Schreyer*
  ICELAND *President Vigdís Finnbogadóttir*

1982
  FINLAND *President and Mrs Mauno Koivisto*

1983
  UNITED KINGDOM *Queen Elizabeth II and Prince Philip*

Peter Wallenberg went along on the state visit to Italy in 1991 and is seen here chivalrously kissing Queen Silvia's hand. The closeness of the Wallenberg Group and the royal family is a source of some controversy in Swedish business circles. Many think the Wallenbergs make too much of their royal connections. But the Palace claim that the king and the queen try to spread any favours around evenly.
PHOTO: ANDERS HOLMSTRÖM 1991

1984
FRANCE *President and Mrs François Mitterrand*

1985
ZAMBIA *President Dr Kenneth Kaunda*
JAPAN *Official Visit Crown Prince Akihito and Crown Princess Michiko*
DENMARK *Queen Margrethe II and Prince Henrik*

1986
ALGERIA *President and Mrs Chadli Bendjedid*

1987
NETHERLANDS *Queen Beatrix and Prince Claus*

1988
WEST GERMANY *Federal President and Baroness Richard von Weizsäcker*

1990

ISRAEL *President and Mrs Chaim Herzog*
PORTUGAL *President and Mrs Mário Soares*

1991
CHECHOSLOVAKIA *President and Mrs Václav Havel*
LUXEMBOURG *Grand Duke Jean and Grand Duchess Joséphine-Charlotte*

1992
NORWAY *King Harald V and Queen Sonja*

1994
FINLAND *President and Mrs Martti Ahtisaari*
BELGIUM *King Albert and Queen Paola*

1995
POLAND *President and Mrs Lech Walesa*
ESTONIA *President and Mrs Lennart Meri*
LATVIA *President Guntis Ulmanis*
LITHUANIA *President Algirdas Brazauskas*

Ulf Adelsohn
SYDSVENSKAN 1986

Johan Nordén
SYDSVENSKAN 1988

Ankie Ramberg
PHOTO: PER BJÖRN 1990

Ajje Philipson
PRESSENS BILD 1972

The queen, the king, Agneta Kihlström and Björn Kreuger
PHOTO: JAN FORSMAN 1976

Fredrik Skiöldebrand and Peter Degermark
PHOTO: CLAS GÖRAN CARLSSON 1974

Johan Beckman, the King and Carli Kleman Jr
PHOTO: CLAS GÖRAN CARLSSON 1974

John Ambler and prince Johann Georg
PRESSENS BILD 1966

Noppe and Gryr
PHOTO: URBAN BRÅDHE 1986

Ulf Dinkelspiel
PHOTO: JAN FORSMAN 1992

Sven Philip-Sörensen
STENBERGS 1968

Anders Lettström and Pia Degermark *PRESSENS BILD 1974*

Björn Åker-
lund
PHOTO:
CLAS
GÖRAN
CARLSSON
1974

Antonia Ax:son
Johnson and prin-
cess Christina
SYDSVENSKAN 1963

Raoul Hamilton
PHOTO: ÅKE
SIVELAND 1979

Erik Lallerstedt
PHOTO: TORBJÖRN
PERSSON 1994

Caroline and Fred Wennerholm *PHOTO: STEFAN LINDBLOM*
1981

FOTO: LEIF R JANSSON 1993

ARAB WORLD IN UPROAR AFTER THE KING'S HEROIC DEED.

Do you remember why the king had to change his dog's name?

In 1976 King Carl Gustaf and Queen Silvia were celebrating their first Christmas as a royal couple with sister Christina and brother-in-law Tosse Magnuson in Villa Beylon, Ulriksdal. After Christmas dinner the presents were handed out and then the king went for an evening stroll with his labrador Ali in the palace grounds. It was minus 15 degrees centigrade and the ground was thick with snow. Suddenly Ali started sniffing in a snowdrift where the king found a young Chinese girl frozen and unconscious.

The king carried the girl the 300 metres to Villa Beylon where they wrapped her in blankets to warm her up. The ambulance and police were called. The Chinese girl's temperature had dropped to 35 degrees centigrade and she had almost frozen to death. She was rushed to Karolinska Hospital where she soon recovered.

The girl's name was Liza Kristiane and she had come straight from Hong Kong to celebrate Christmas with a Swedish friend living in one of the research wings of the Ulriksdal Palace.

After celebrating Christmas, Liza was suddenly taken with the idea of finding out what Swedish snow was like. She went out alone into the freezing night to "play in the snow", obviously failed to cope with the intense cold and collapsed in the snow drift where the king and Ali found her and saved her life.

The story of the frozen Chinese girl and the king's "heroic" deed was cabled out all over the world and gained a lot of attention.

Not least in the Arab world, where they took sharp exception to the Swedish king calling a dumb animal such as a dog by the name of Ali – a holy name and a title of some distinction to the Muslims.

Shocked letters poured into the Swedish royal house from the whole Arab world. The pressure became so great that the king in the end had to calm the Muslims down by renaming Ali.

To Charlie.

The little prince's nanny Nenne Björnberg tells us that as a little boy he craved affection and loved to be cuddled. Here we see him fondling "his" pekinese on a sofa at the Royal Palace in Stockholm. *PHOTO: ARTHUR STRONG 1950*

WERE YOU TO INVITE THE KING TO DINNER.

If you were to invite the king to dinner there are a few little extra things you need to think about. First make sure in good time that the king can really come. If his reply is yes then send out invitation cards to the other guests writing "Time: 18.55" to make it clear that the royal couple will be there and that other guests should already be there when they arrive. Nobody may arrive after the royals. This ancient royal tradition is defended by the Palace on practical grounds. The royal couple are the guests of honour.

By arriving first other guests have time to greet each other. By arriving last the royal couple gives them the time to do so. Then when the king and the queen arrive, they can greet all the guests and that way everyone gets to the table quicker. So says the Palace.

Etiquette also demands that nobody goes home before the royal couple.

The king's reputation as a hardened night-owl is well-known so this rule of etiquette sometimes causes problems. The king stays and stays, getting livelier and happier the longer the evening goes on. Meanwhile other guests however get sleepier or have baby sitters wanting to go home, but should still avoid sneaking away before the royal couple.

They do anyway of course! Eventually it is three or four in the morning, the host and hostess are falling asleep but the king, without even coming up for air, calmly continues sipping his whisky – once upon a time it was Scotch but now it is said that the Irish "goes down better" – and suddenly only a handful of guests remain.

Now the situation becomes truly embarrassing because slipping out discreetly is no longer an option. The king with his iron constitution may even decide to continue partying at a nightclub. Many an exhausted lady friend of the royal couple with small children asleep at home remembers how they admired Queen Silvia as she accompanied her festive spouse.

– She is incredibly loyal! It can be two o'clock in the morning and pouring with rain, but Silvia goes along as well. After official dinners the king prefers to talk standing up. For hours on end.

– The king just stands and stands. People are going down like ninepins but the king carries on standing, scarcely noticing the exhaustion all around him. He really does have an iron constitution, bemoan many reporters.

The king's friends know that he loves to dress up and so they arrange "18th century" fancy dress parties or "Charter Trip to Rio" theme evenings.

At private functions the security services call up the king's hosts ahead of time to agree on whether aides or bodyguards are to be invited to the dinner. It is not always necessary but Sweden's Intelligence Services keep a check on his movements as the government must always know where the king is. There are no welcoming speeches at private dinners because otherwise the king would have to respond with a thank-you speech. As the guest of honour, the king always accompanies the hostess to the table

185

This golden egg cup always stands by the king's place when he gives a dinner at the palace. The tradition originated in Karl XIV Johan's time. The French Bernadotte was worried about the strange Swedish food so he always wanted to have an egg in reserve. The egg cup is part of the "state cutlery", a nine-part set signed by Gustav Folcker in 1828. *PHOTO: ALEXIS DAFLOS 1995*

186

"To this the royal couple never say no..." The king always enjoys the academic setting in Lund and when the academic society celebrated its 150th anniversary they raised the roof off. The guests were entertained by the royal couple toasting each other with the classic song duet "For it was in our youth's fairest springtime...". From the left, Queen Silvia, AF-chairman, Professor Hampus Lyttkens, Elly Hörjel, university rector Nils Stjernquist, AF's ombudsman Britt-Marie Hesselbom and associate professor Martin Weibull. To the right of the king can be glimpsed provincial governor Nils Hörjel and a first lady of the court Alice Trolle-Wachmeister. To the left of the king sits the university chancellor Carl Gustaf Andrén. *PHOTO: PER LINDSTRÖM 1980*

and would have no chance to relax if his whole time were spent holding thank-you speeches.

On the other hand he sometimes asks to say a few words. The style is witty and informal, a world apart from his official speeches.

Nobody need be overanxious about food and drink. Peppered confit of duck or sophisticated soufflés are really not essential. Surprisingly perhaps, the king is not the slightest bit fussy and actually likes simple day-to-day fare.

But the food must be good! And the wine right. A tasty pasta sauce and lightly grilled herring fillets will put him in just as good a mood as a tender venison steak or a spicy hot-pot. Mind you, brown sauce is not popular. And he is sick and tired of coffee, except when taken with liqueurs or out of a thermos flask up on the fells. Everybody in his circle of acquaintances is surprised how the king keeps himself so slim with all the marvellous food he is offered.

His – and the queen's – secret is to be hap-

py enough to taste everything as a courtesy to their hosts, but to avoid taking seconds. Perhaps they also pick discreetly at that last bit under the salad.

– The king looks damn good, slim and incredibly well-dressed. He has a really nice body for hanging a suit on and I am green with envy, sighs a grey-suited member of Sweden's establishment.

The king is very careful not to express an opinion about his favourite food or his favourite wine. He would only have to breathe a word about fillet of beef provençale being his favourite for instance and he would probably end up eating it all the time.

And should he but murmur that he pre-

fers red wine to white, the importers of white wine would be struggling for business.

The king might consider signing an official or a private guest book provided the royal couple are given a whole page to themselves. But do not ask the king for his autograph! He never gives it. If he did he would never do anything else.

Many people comment on how different our down-to-earth and unsnobbish royal family is compared to the English royal house. Elizabeth, her children and grandchildren have beeen brought up according to strict court etiquette to be really royal and far removed from ordinary people. Crown Prince Charles for example never sleeps in the

Welcome to the table. The royal couple invite government ministers and the retiring prime minister Ingvar Carlsson to lunch in the dining room at Drottningholm Palace after the first informatory cabinet meeting of the year. *PHOTO: LEIF R JANSSON 1996*

sheets provided by others when he travels away. He packs his own royal crested palace sheets, or rather his aides do.

– Our king would never dream of doing so. He despises snobbery, hates fuss and would never think of himself as anybody remarkable, loyal Swedish courtiers assure us.

What if you yourself were invited to dinner with the king? The chance is of course quite high if you are an ambassador, a director-general, professor, top military brass or somebody in the world of art and culture. But there is also hope for us ordinary citizens. Although we have to really earn it.

Apart from formal dinners on state visits, dinner for parliament and the Nobel prize dinner, the royal couple normally arrange three "royal invitation dinners" each spring. Last spring there were only two because preparations for Victoria's university entrance examination and for the king's 50th birthday took up a lot of time. There were also rumours of economy measures. Normally 160 guests are invited to each of these royal functions. Even if much of the guest list

chooses itself (new director-generals, ambassadors, new appointments to the top of the civil service, organisations and industry etc.) there are always a few places reserved for the royal couple's own personal guests.

Provincial governors provide the royal couple with tips on people who have made their mark on local provincial life in some way, for instance. So ordinary citizens who would never have expected a royal invitation may still receive one.

The royal couple play an active part in choosing the guests and the menu. It so happened that it was the king, for instance, who decided to invite Ingemar Stenmark, Abba and Lill-Babs to the palace. These dinners are formal occasions calling for tails and long dress. The pattern never changes.

Guests gather (in good time!) in "Vita Havet" (The White Sea) with its flaming log fires and scented flowers. Exactly at 19.30 the royal couple arrive and greet their guests for ten minutes. Five minutes are allowed for the guests to proceed into dinner, laid out on the 44.5 metre long table in Karl XI's gallery, by way of the Don Quixote room and the Sofia Magdalena state bedroom.

Guests are given an hour and a quarter at the table to get through five courses. No speeches except for state visits. A minute-by-minute schedule ensures that the kitchen staff and the 45 waiters in their black livery coats and yellow knee breeches can function efficiently.

The table is immaculately laid with nothing out of line. The trick is to stretch out a long piece of string the whole length of the table before laying out the glasses and cutlery and place settings and straightening the chairs into neat rows.

There are a number of little curiosities at the dinner table. The Brazilian silver service for instance was inherited from Oskar I's Queen Josefina and was so valuable that it was shipped to Sweden aboard an armed warship for safety's sake.

Karl XIV Johan's little gold egg cup is always part of the king's place setting. Not because the king is particularly fond of eggs but because his French predecessor wanted an egg in reserve in case he did not like the strange Swedish food.

There is usually a small piece of Swedish crisp bread by each guest's place to nibble at between courses.

If you are new in your job or picked out for some other reason, a little note may lie by your place specifying an exact time when the king and queen wish to have a word with you after dinner. This gives you a chance to think up some interesting topic of conversation from within your field.

After dinner everyone spreads out in Vita Havet, Don Quixote and Sofia Magdalena. The guests stand up drinking their coffee while the king and the queen converse with the note recipients, ushered forward – preferably – to the minute by Palace officials. Dinner finishes at 23.00 after which it is limousine jam in the inner courtyard.

Often the king and queen become so interested in their conversations with their selected guests that the timetable breaks down. The king once tried to extend the schedule to 23.20, but was told it was not possible as the international diplomatic custom was for everybody to go home at 23.00. Disappointed guests, who did not have time to meet the royal couple, no doubt think that the king ought to have got his way.

The royal couple's invitation dinners are greatly coveted and many Swedes would, as with the Nobel Dinner, give anything to be there just once in their life.

HOW IS THE KING TO KEEP POVERTY FROM THE CASTLE GATE?

When the king was a schoolboy in Sigtuna he had ten kronor a week pocket money. Today he has rather more and according to the estimates of some economic journalists is worth about 157 million kronor in private wealth, placed in Swedish shares, unit trusts, bonds and property. The king's own palace Solliden is not included in this calculation of his fortune.

Like all other citizens the king has to declare his income and pay tax. And like nearly everybody else he makes plans for old age and pays into a private pension fund.

It is always being pointed out just how poor our Swedish royal house is compared with its European counterparts. While the Swedish king has a fortune of about 157 million kronor – and the right to use eight palaces – England's Queen Elizabeth is sitting on 60 000 million kronor and the Dutch Queen Beatrix on 29 000 million kronor. And the Sultan of Brunei is in a different league altogether being worth 300 000 million kronor.

In recent years estimates of Queen Elizabeth's fortune have been reduced on the grounds that the enormous number of art treasures in her palaces and castles are not actually her personal property but belong to the British crown. But even without the art treasures Elizabeth still ranks seventeenth among the wealthiest in the land. Our king just about scrapes into the top 100 richest Swedes.

The king's fortune breaks down like this:

Swedish shares	80–100 million kr
Unit trusts	20 million kr
Bonds	10 million kr
Property (Skeppsbron)	25 million kr
Summer house	1 million kr
Boats/cars	1 million kr
Total	137–157 million kr

His share portfolio normally contains safe shares in Swedish export companies (preferably Wallenberg): Electrolux, Ericsson, Astra, Asea, SKF and SE-Banken. Share prices rise and fall and in recent years the value of the king's shares have fluctuated between 80 and 100 million kronor.

The king is hardly a big player on the stock market, but is interested enough to follow the share prices and reads the financial press. He does not make dramatic changes to his portfolio and always takes the advice of his chief steward Bengt Telland who looks after the king's finances nowadays and previously wor-

The king has eight royal palaces at his disposal with the Royal Palace in Stockholm the largest. In addition he owns Solliden and has the leasehold for Stenhammar. There is of course a lot to maintain and look after, but here it is not palace maintenance that brought the king out onto the roof but a photographer who wanted to take a beautiful picture of the king and Stockholm. *PHOTO: LEIF ENGBERG 1995*

SVERIGE

10 kr

C.G. CARLSSON/L.S   1996   CZ.SLANIA sc.

On one of the 50th birthday commemorative stamps Carl Gustaf is standing in the Bernadotte Gallery in the Royal Palace in Stockholm with François Gerard's painting of his French predecessor Karl XIV Johan in the background.

Each year December 10th is ringed in red in the king's diary. This is when the ceremonial distribution of the Nobel prizes takes place in Stockholm's Concert Hall with a gala dinner afterwards in the City Hall's Blue Hall, a festive occasion watched by millions of TV viewers, many dreaming of attending just once in their life. In 1992 the English speaking poet Derek Walcott from St. Lucia in the West Indies received the Nobel Prize for Literature from the Swedish king. *PHOTO: LEIF R JANSSON 1992*

"HUR MAN LYCKAS I AFFÄRER
UTAN ATT EGENTLIGEN ANSTRÄNGA SIG"

OSCARS-TEATERN

In his younger days Carl Gustaf had time to go to the theatre and even looked in on the dressing rooms afterwards. Here he meets with the leading players Jarl Kulle and Anna Sundqvist in "How to Succeed in Business.." at Oscars in Stockholm.

PHOTO: SVEN-ÅKE PERS-SON 1964

ked with trust business and wealth management at SE-Banken. When it comes to placement of shares, the king does of course prefer to invest in environmental companies.

In the financial press columns by the mile have been written about the king's poor property deals. In 1989 when property in the centre of Stockholm was at its absolute dearest, the king took purchased Skeppsbron 24 immediately below the palace for 38 million kronor.

It was considered a good deal at the time but then came the crash in the property market and the property's value plummeted. Today it is reckoned to be worth between 20 and 25 million kronor. In other words the king would make a thumping loss if he were to sell the property today. But why should he when he can wait patiently for better times?

Elisabeth Tarras-Wahlberg, head of information at the Palace, takes the king's domestic affairs as an example of how difficult it can be for the Palace to deny rumours. When the king set about buying the property in 1989 it was hot news for the media who immediately interpreted the purchase as part of the king's plans for Crown Princess Victoria's future. Victoria would live there on Skeppsbron near the palace, the media decided.

– At that time the king needed to restructure his investments. The whole thing was just a financial deal with nothing whatsoever to do with Victoria or any other considerations relating to the accommodation of the royal children, Elisabeth Tarras-Wahlberg explains.

– But it has been absolutely impossible to convince the media of this! You only have to give the matter a little thought and it is obvious the royal family have plenty of other housing options for their children so buying a particular building for this purpose was quite unnecessary. Besides, where would be the sense in buying so far ahead, long before the children were ready to leave home.

In addition to the privately owned Solliden and the leasehold of Stenhammar the king has the use of eight other palaces. Obviously one of these would have been suitable as student digs, Ulriksdal for instance which is almost empty and situated close to town. Less well-known is Storlien, a sports cottage in Tärnaby inherited from King Gustav VI Adolf and included in the king's private fortune together with the cars and boats at a combined value of 2 million kronor.

Solliden on Öland is a significant item in the king's fortune but here the media seems to run out of imagination. Nobody knows how to value it and so Solliden is usually left out of the calculation. Counting Solliden, the king's fortune would be considerably more.

The boats, yes, these include his favourite, the motor boat Ancylus built by Fairline and an old rebuilt motor torpedo boat. And in the palace stables stand several of the king's own cars (BMW and Volvo), some classic cars (a 1959 Daimler and a 1969 Cadillac Fleetwood) alongside some real horse power in the shape of twenty well-groomed horses.

The most recent Palace budget amounted to 107 million kronor but with the change in the budget system this allocation will have to last a year and a half.

Of this 107 million, most goes to maintenance and running costs for the royal palaces, with about 45 million going tax-free as 18 months of "apanage" (from the Latin apanare = to provide with bread). 70% of the apanage allocation goes to pay the Palace wage bill, leaving 10–11 million kronor to cover the royal family's representation costs (where wage bills are also woven in), travel (the foreign office contributes towards state visits), maintenance of cars, the royal stables, clothing, household and his 50th birthday party.

The king does not receive a salary but he does get some cost-free benefits. He lives rent free in Drottningholm and can personally determine how the eight palaces are to be used. He has access to large tracts of hunting estates that would cost ordinary hunters annual fees of at least four or five million kronor. And his constant companion and right-hand man, his personal aide, is on free secondment from the armed forces.

Myths have been circulating from as far back as the old king's reign that the Swedish royal house is impoverished, receives a pitiful allowance and has so little money from the tax payer that the poor unfortunate king has to dip into his own pocket to make ends meet.

But if things have been tight in the past, then for the royal family, just as for the rest of us, the future will be tougher. Spending on the king and his court is being slashed just as savagely as the rest of government spending and he is under strict instructions to take a knife, if not a chain saw, and pare back even further. The 1995/96 budget calls for a 5.4 million kronor cut-back in the king's 1998 budget. In Autumn 1995 the magazine Månadens Affärer (Business Monthly) came up with a way of keeping poverty from the castle gate: sell all the property managed by the Djurgården commissioners.

The state owns the land but the Djurgården commissioners, the king's estate management company, holds the right to lease it out, as well as owning the 20 000 cubic metres of buildings and 10 000 cubic metres of living space on the 1 000 hectare tract of land from Gröna Lund in the south to Brunnsviken in the north. Selling these properties alone could raise as much as 500 million kronor the magazine estimated. There is only one flaw in the magazine's proposal. According to legal opinion the Djurgården commissioners would be breaking the law if they tried to sell off the buildings.

The king always has an aide in his company when on either official or private business. Included in the staff are twelve aides, each highly-skilled, outgoing, good at languages and hand-picked from the highest ranks of the military. They are on secondment from the armed forces and each works as the king's aide for a month at a time. Nobody is as close to the royal family as the aide who accompanies the king at Drottningholm, the Palace, Solliden and Storlien and on all his travel and official engagements. The aide is with the king in his car, boat and plane, on the ski trail and jogging paths and in the theatre stalls and processions and more besides. The aide must be familiar with the king's schedule, all the times, the meetings, transport, the placing for the royal couple, when they should go home and so on. It is also the aide who looks after money and steps in to pay for the king if necessary. Perhaps the king would like a hot dog on his way home from a gala dinner.

The king is an honorary doctor at Sweden's Agricultural University, Stockholm's Institute of Technology and Åbo Academy in Finland.

The Only Place
For Kings is
in a Pack of Cards.

To question the monarchy is rather like swearing in church, almost worse. Swedes in general love their monarchy and their royal family with an ardour which surprised chief editors are compelled to take notice of each time their newspaper says something negative about the monarchy or the monarch.

There is a storm of popular protest, a roar of anguish from deep in the Swedish heart. Editorial offices are inundated with phone calls from distressed citizens pleading: do not mess with our royal family!

Currently in the 90s, with a lively, charming and attractive royal family in full bloom at Drottningholm few Swedes are campaigning for a republic.

But it has not always been like this. In 1954 Republikanska Klubben (RK) was founded to sweep away the monarchy and turn Sweden into a republic.

Hans Haste was persuaded by Ivar Öhman, the driving force behind "Folket I Bild" (People Illustrated) to be the first chairman of Sweden's Republican Club. Haste was succeeded by the editor Sten Sjöberg, who admitted in 1984 that RK was dying and only being kept alive by a board of pensioners.

RK does not exist any more even though many members are still alive and certainly still bear the republican battle cry deep in their lukewarm, or perhaps even their hot, hearts.

Here is a long list of RK members from 1977:

Eva Moberg, Per Wrigstad, Jan Myrdal, Gertrud Sigurdsen, Ingemar Mundebo, Elon Johansson, Mats Hulth, Åke Rangborg, Pia Brandelius, Barbro Engman, Roine Carlsson, Hans-Göran Franck, Bo E Åkermark, Björn Kumm etc.

It was no coincidence that RK was founded in the 50s. After the death of the old king Gustav V, the media began delving into the homosexual goings-on around the palace. And in the wake of the Kejne and Haijby affairs and several cases of corruption the idea of abolishing the monarchy fell on fertile soil.

There was also a sort of vacuum created by the gap in the succession following the death of the heir to the throne Gustav Adolf in an air crash in 1947. With a relatively elderly monarch Gustav VI Adolf on the throne and a young child Carl Gustaf as his successor in some hazy distant future, the republicans thought that the time for the republic had come.

In 1954 a statutory committee of enquiry was set up to prepare the ground for a com-

Carl XVI Gustaf beside a real fairy tale crown in front of the Royal Palace in Stockholm. Sweden's actual royal crown was made in 1561 for Erik XIV and is kept nowadays in the Treasury. Oskar II was the last king to be crowned. *PHOTO: KENT HULT 1993*

plete revision of the 1809 constitution which had become hopelessly outdated. The constitution stated that "the King alone shall govern the realm". But this bore little resemblance to the real world emerging from the breakthrough of parliamentary democracy. Government and parliament actually ruled the realm.

During his 43 years on the throne King Gustav V had occasionally bolstered his position with constitutional arguments in order to maintain his personal power as king. Government and parliament could rely on a more democratic attitude from Gustav VI Adolf, but they still wanted the constitution to reflect the fact that the people ruled Sweden and not the king.

It took nearly 20 years to change the constitution. But finally in the new legislation which came into force in 1975 the king's power was swept away in no uncertain terms.

The point was hammered home in the very first paragraph in the statement that "all public power derives from the people", meaning the people represented in parliament. The king remained as head of state but had been stripped of his power and was left as a mere figure-head with purely representative functions.

But during the 50s, 60s and to a certain degree the 70s, the republican hounds were still baying. The republic did not have to look like Finland or the USA with a strong president elected by the people, but the president could instead function more like a speaker looking after representative duties without wielding any real power.

The Republican Club organised debates, published a newspaper "Republiken" and tried in every way it could to create a climate of opinion for a republic.

The highest point was a debate in Stockholm's consert hall where there was a clash between Herbert Tingsten and the then Conservative Party leader Jarl Hjalmarson. The author Sven Stolpe reviewed from the ringside.

While RK members were duplicating their stencils in a murky cellar behind Norra Bantorget, the little fair-haired prince was growing up into a happy young man with a sense of fun and plenty of glamour.

He had his serious side and this was on view at the state opening of parliament each year and on other occasions. But even more visible was the young man with a cigarette in his mouth in the pages of the weekly gossip magazines steering his erratic course between Alexandra's night club in Stockholm and wild holidays in the Alps or on the Riviera.

With such pictures of the young Tjabbe imprinted on the public mind, the baying of the hounds arose once again as RK decried the undemocratic nature of the monarchy and demanded a republic as soon as possible.

The Social Democrats had – and still have – the demand for a republic written into their party manifesto but not a peep was heard on the subject for fear of losing voters. Nancy Eriksson, Valter Åman and some others piped up but only to be dismissed by the party leaders with the claim that "the question of a republic is not on the agenda at present".

At the beginning of the 70s smoke from another explosion threatened to blow across Swedish society with the radical left of 1968 and its student uprising culminating in the occupation of the student union and the violent and long drawn out strikes around the LKAB mines in Kiruna.

Militant students, flower-power hippies, ordinary workers and the media made common cause against the establishment. The wave swept across Swedish society from the left and shook it to its foundations.

The Palace responded by trying to slam the gate on the left. The pictures of the partying Tjabbe were to be rubbed out and replaced by images of a powerless but serious-minded king. He talked with the trade union workers and studied immigrant education in Hallonbergen. He even signed his royal decrees with a red ball point pen given him by the unions – a symbolic synthesis of Swedish social democracy and monarchy.

In the 70s the mood for a republic began to shift slowly in Sweden. When the new constitution abolished the power of the king, the republicans consoled themselves with that. And prime minister Olof Palme calmed matters further by suggesting that the monarchy could be removed "at the stroke of a pen" if necessary.

The republicans calmed down and were given good cause to bury the hatchet for good (?) by the king's choice of queen, the sunny fairy tale wedding of 1976 and the increasingly serious image the king projected over the years. Then when three well-behaved royal children were born and one after another secured the succession for the foreseeable future, friends of the republicans told them their demands had been met. The last sign of life from the Republican Club was in 1984.

In 1989 Expressen published a supplement on the king with the theme "Our king is now man enough for his throne" and Dagens Nyheter commented in a full-page spread two years later that "the king now fits his suit" noting that King Carl Gustaf seemed to be a stable and ambitious person who had not had everything handed to him on a plate.

Today Carl XVI Gustaf sits secure on his throne. The media may still report the king's gaffes and unfortunate remarks but he is much admired and has a wide-spread popularity.

In recent years, when asked "which living Swede do you admire the most?" the public opinion polls have answered by placing King Carl Gustaf at number one (closely followed by Carl Bildt, Jerzy Einhorn and Percy Barnevik).

It is remarked quite often that the Bernadottes mature late. But in researching this book it was suggested in several interviews that the king's maturing process is still going on and that within a few years, once he feels more secure in his role as king and dares to relax a little, he will come to be every bit as popular as his grandfather Gustav VI Adolf.

Their starting points were certainly different. Gustav VI Adolf was nearly 68 when he inherited the throne. He had long since ceased to question his own worth and was generally respected.

King Carl Gustaf on the other hand was only 27 when he took over as king. He was uncertain of himself after being rushed through his society education and ceremonies at a speed which hardly allowed him to catch his breath or digest the information stuffed into him. Many people believe that had he been allowed to take things more easily in the beginning he would have grown into his king's mantle more quickly.

A close observer who has known the king for 15 years says:

– It is exciting to live with a person who is changing. During the time I have known the king, he has developed constantly and become more and more at ease. But the king never unwinds on official occasions and this is a pity because if he did, people would come to see what a fundamentally nice person he is.

While researching this book, royalists were more willing than republicans to subject themselves to the ordeal of an interview. But here anyway are two conversations with representatives of the opposing camps.

Gustav Vasa may not be one of the king's ancestors but Carl Gustaf is following in his predecessor's footsteps nonetheless. In 1977 he took part in the annual Vasaloppet much to the delight of the media. In 1987 he took part again.
PHOTO: KENT ÖSTLUND 1977

Elof Rörvall, chairman of the royalist society, which works to strengthen the constitutional monarchy in Sweden. After public appearances by the royal family the society's membership always increases. *PHOTO: KENT HULT 1996*

Growing royalist battalions

Royalism thrives in the little Stockholm suburb of Hökmossen. Here lives Elof Rörvall, chairman of Rojalistiska Föreningen (RojF), The Society of Royalists, Sweden's only country-wide society for royalists, ie. supporters of the monarchy.

RojF was founded in 1979 and its purpose is to "widen and strengthen the constitutional monarchy in Sweden as an indispensable part of tradition and governance". The society has members all over Sweden and has no ideological or party political affiliations.

Today's membership stands at 1200 surging ahead every time there is a TV debate between royalists and republicans.

– When the republicans appear on TV, led by "that woman in the red dress", as my wife and I call her (Aftonbladet journalist Anette Kullenberg), then membership normally increases by 30 or 40, Elof Rörvall comments contentedly.

Occasions like Crown Princess Victoria's Coming of Age and the queen's 50th birthday also swell the membership register.

RojF does not have an active programme to gain members, with campaigns, special offers and the like. It has neither the money nor the people.

– We work with very modest means with most members coming to us through friends and acquaintances. I myself was introduced to RojF by the then chairman and my predecessor Lars Laurin whom I met in the "Men of 1917" society.

Elof, 78 years old, is a former police chief who had responsibility for security and traffic during royal events. The first time was in 1950 when Gustav V was lying in state at the palace.

– But I met him once at the end of his life when he came to attend the ceremony around the moving of the High Court to Riddarhustorget, Elof recounts.

– Then King Gustav V was quite frail and we sneaked him up in a service lift at the back of the magnificent old building. It was too hard for him to climb the stairs.

After his police time Elof Rörvall became

managing director of Svenska Korpidrottför-bundet (SKIF) and has met many of the royal family through his sports activities which include rowing, skating and skiing.

– In the beginning of the 40s I met the then Crown Prince Gustav Adolf at a rowing regatta and he came along in his trench coat and said "hej, hej". He was a man of the people, that one.

– Even more so and really nice is of course Prince Bertil who I have met on many occasions including the 1976 USA tour and when he helped us open "Skridskor till tusen" (Skates for All) on Gärdet in the 1970s.

Elof met our current King Carl Gustaf when, as a little prince, he used to run around on Södra Djurgården. And more recently in connection with the king's wedding in 1976.

On that occasion I was invited as the representative of the SKIF and found it all very fine and rather splendid being there.

Elof Rörvall is also active working with victims of crime and has been to the palace to brief the king and queen about his work.

– The king asked me a lot of questions, but the queen was even more curious!

At the home of a chairman of royalists I thought there would be lots of items like crowns and flags and royal portraits. But in the tidy little house I glimpsed only one portrait of Carl Gustaf and Silvia, discreetly hung next to the bookshelf and bought by Elof himself.

It is the only sign of royalty I could find. Apart from paper serviettes with crowns on with the coffee.

– Although we do have much nicer ones at our summer place with the royal coat of arms, Elof confessed.

I had also expected an ardent fan of the king. Does Elof love the king?

– I have never really thought about it. But nor do I need to think in those terms, he replies thoughtfully.

– All I will say is that it would be most unfortunate for our country if the monarchy were to fall, he added firmly.

In other words Elof Rönvall is a well-balanced and sober-minded royalist whose affection is directed more towards the monarchy than towards the king himself. It is confidence in the monarchy as a stabilising force for the country that has led Elof to devote four years of his life to being chairman of RojF.

– Even if the monarchy has little power, the king still represents stability. And the royal couple can really charm the most fervent republican.

But back to the society of royalists. What exactly do they do?

The country is divided into seven regions and each arranges its own events. Skåne has just been given its own region. The Stockholm region is the most active, inviting members to lectures, conferences and study visits.

Last autumn we showed a long video of Victoria's 18th birthday. In December each year we celebrate Oscar Day with a regional dinner and then we have a little ceremony where we light candles in front of a portrait of the royal couple and sing the King's Song of course.

Some members take part in the 6th of June National Day parade bearing the RojF standard and flag.

Telegrams to the royal family are popular. Congratulations telegrams were sent on Victoria's 18th birthday and on Princess Lilian's 80th birthday.

– And we also sent a get-well telegram to Prince Bertil. Each time RojF has their annual general meeting they send a telegram to the royal couple and reverently read out the thank-you telegram from them.

RojF's purpose is to spread increased awareness about the monarchical form of government, its historic roots and its current standing, it says in the society's rules. They also follow what goes on in parliament and keep abreast of other public debates on Sweden's form of governance.

As soon as any malicious journalist writes anything negative about the royal family, RojF turns out in their defence in the pages of its own magazine "Rojalisten", published four times a year.

It is a well produced and neatly presented magazine that provides an accurate account of flag days, the royal couple's programme, new Palace appointments, royal telegrams sent and received and so on.

But it gets worked up when Rörvall as the publisher and the other contributors charge into the fray, objecting to the king being called a "little royal Scrooge", refuting insinuations that Queen Silvia is poorly educated or attacking the tabloid journalist Ulf Nilson for his comments on TV that the king's position was ridiculous and the king himself poorly informed.

204

– Just think if ordinary citizens were given the same vicious treatment as the king. They would immediately sue for libel! But the royal couple cannot even comment on such lies. I really suffer with the royal couple both as a royalist and as a retired police chief who knows something about the way people react to abuse, Elof Rörvall explains.

In several places in its various issues, Rojalisten states that 80% of the Swedish people want to retain the monarchy. How does it know that?

– It's confirmed in every opinion poll!

RojF write mainly for themselves, ie in

After the ceremony in the Great Hall Carl Gustaf, as the newly crowned king, accepts the cheers from the waiting crowds outside the palace. He was very happy and moved and perhaps he would have waved a little extra if he had known his faithful old nanny Nenne Björnberg was standing in the midst of the throng, shedding a tear of emotion and pride for "her" prince who had now become king.
PHOTO: URBAN BRÅDHE 1973

Rojalisten. Elof has learned over the years that there is little point in trying to get "corrections" printed in the mainstream press. But the king does make howlers from time to time. And surely the media should report them?

Elof's mouth tightens.

– May I respond to that with my own question? Should we not have the right to make a slip of the tongue if we quickly correct it? Everybody says things wrong now and again.

Membership in RojF costs 125 kronor a year and family membership is 75 kronor. The money is used for various member events. There are only a small number of sponsors.

At the moment they are organising a trip to the Bernadotte roots in Pau, France. Last year they took a trip to Vadstena.

There is no international cooperation, although there are similar societies in England, Portugal, Spain, Estonia and Bulgaria(!).

Through their magazine, RojF members can buy items with the RojF logo, the royal couple's initials with a crown on top.

There are postcards, membership badges and rubber stamps with the words "Strengthen the Monarchy". These are also sold at the little office on Barnängsgatan.

And the members themselves?

Mostly middle class. The poor and the really rich are not members. But there are plenty of teachers, engineers, policemen, lawyers, civil servants, doctors and the like.

– We have some chauffeurs, a furniture shop assistant and, perhaps not surprisingly, a former guide at the Royal Palace.

Even if the age profile is high, the new members are mostly "youngsters" under 50.

– We do not attract the 22–23 year olds, Elof Rönvall says. But he does not think this an indication of Swedish royalism dying out.

– It would be an enormous tragedy for Sweden if the monarchy collapsed. But I see no risk of that whatsoever at the moment!

Per Edström has campaigned for a republic for decades, but is still not convinced that the country would be any better ruled with one. It makes little difference whether an elected president or a king inheriting a throne sits at the top. What matters is altering the way of governing so that all of us participate in decisions. *PHOTO: KENT HULT 1995*

206

Declining republican brigades

The place for a symbol such as a king is in a pack of cards, not in society at large!

The theatre-boat Arena's legendary founder-producer, actor Per Edström is very firm in his anti-royalism.

In 1996 he was the only active republican without a party card we were able to find in the Swedish kingdom. Per Edström pursues his struggle for a republic as the chairman of Sailing Club RS. RS stands for "Republikanska Seglare" (Republican Sailors).

Sailing Club RS was founded in 1967 as a counterweight to the Royal Swedish Sailing Club KSSS ("Kungliga Svenska Segel Sällskapet").

Per Edström is a 70 year old "hyss Emil" (mischievous Emil) character straight from Astrid Lindgren's book. Ever since the 1930s he has been an outspoken opponent of the monarchy, fighting for a republic.

– It was quite something in the 60s when RS got going, he recalls.

When Per Edström and his republican sailing friends applied for membership of the Swedish Yachting Association under the name of Republikanska Seglare, they were turned down by the venerable institution.

– The association regarded our club as political and they were afraid that clubs with names like "Neo-Nazi Sailing Club" would spring up if RS were allowed membership. And how would that look?

The Swedish Sports Council were of the same opinion and came to a solemn decision in 1969 that "the Swedish Sports Council no longer accepts clubs with prefixes such as "royal" to their name".

– When Sweden's sports world would not accept either "royal" or "republican" clubs, we decided at our AGM in 1970 to change the name to Sailing Club RS.

The cunning republican sailors expected to be turned down again since the initials RS still stood for republican sailors. But the yachting association unexpectedly turned a blind eye.

– And we have not been kicked out yet, although we make no secret of our allegiance and always sail flying the blue republican ensign with a big yellow sun on it.

An artist-member Svenolov Ehrén designed the flag and it sells at cost price for 50 kronor. At one RS annual general meeting there was a big discussion about having a republican red sun instead of a yellow one, but the proposal was voted down.

– And can you believe that once a particularly uptight KSSS member, on seeing our flag, dropped his pants on deck and presented us with his bare rump as he sailed past. As a demonstration against republics presumably!

The RS office is out on Värmdö in Per Edström's mildly crazy house with its barn, studio, workshop, winter garden (with fish pond), theatre, typesetting room, solar panels, modern computer office and carpentry shed.

A rigid order rules in this seeming chaos with all tools, files, papers and historical facts in their right place. Edström scurries around like a retriever fetching flags, t-shirts, club papers and agendas, always finding exactly what he is after.

High up under the ceiling hangs a magnificent crested coat of arms with the words "By Royal Appointment – Suppliers to The King".

– That is the RS challenge trophy handed out to the RS member who drops the worst clanger of the year, something like coming last in a race, going about badly or showing up at a royal dinner by mistake.

– My little brother Lars (Edström, the theatre director) actually did that. He won the challenge trophy that year but was then promptly slung out of RS.

– I have never been invited to a royal dinner and wouldn't go if I were. Absolutely no reason to, big brother Per assured me firmly.

RS also awards an honorary prize to the person who has done the most for the republican cause.

Last year's winner of the prize statuette was the Aftonbladet journalist Anette Kullenberg "because she made a stand against the monarchy and wrote her articles in Aftonbladet".

Out of a dusty box Per pulls the official grey and blue RS t-shirt with the words "Republikanska Seglare" on it.

– Olof Palme was given a t-shirt when he was a member of the society. He was a member well into the 70s. He wore it under his jacket one summer when he went to a cabinet meeting at Sofiero where the old king was living.

– But he wore it back to front so that the words "Republikanska Seglare" came at the back and couldn't be seen under his jacket. He didn't dare, not straight out in front of the king.

Sailing Club RS is not very big, perhaps 150 members.

Broadly speaking the membership is the same as when RS was founded: Tore Hallén, Janne Sundfeldt, Ramon Fridén, Svenolov Ehrén...

– Vilhelm Moberg and his daughter Eva Moberg were never members of RS, but he helped us name a boat "Sofia Perowska" after a famous Soviet anarchist. When Ville died the spirit went out of the republican debate in Sweden.

Why is Per Edström a republican?

– It is about the way society is governed, he says and fetches a picture with colourful figures in a pyramid and the king at the top.

– The king sits at the top of a hierarchical system which holds him aloft as a powerful symbol. As long as we have this symbol over us in our social system, anybody lower down in the hierarchy, any little upstart bureaucrat, feels secure and excuses himself with the line that "I am innocent, somebody else has decided and they will take responsibility".

The picture says please turn over. On the other side is a completely different picture of society, Per Edström's dream picture:

– Here the figures are arranged in a kind of swirl indicating a more anarchic picture of society. Everybody participates and has influence.

– I am rather proud of this picture. It was painted for Olof Palme, but sadly I never had the chance to hand it over to him before his death.

Per Edström is worried that the fuss about the prizes and the republican flag on the stern of his members' boats may undermine the serious intent behind RS.

– Sailing is a normal and essential part of all our members' lives, so it is our republican beliefs that made us establish Sailing Club RS.

For Per Edström the silly games and the legalistic wranglings around the establishment of RS 30 years ago were indicative of the forces opposing a republic and obstructing the attainment of a society with "greater equality of decision-making".

Mind you, it is not actually a republic as such that is the goal. The only real difference between a monarchy and a republic is that it sets an elected president at the top of the heap instead of a king on a throne. Per Edström sighs deeply. This is not easy.

– It is not at all certain that it would be better with a republic. But there must be a change in the whole way of governing. So everybody can take part in making decisions.

– Perhaps it must be an anarchist society...and we are rather anarchist in RS... but I've seen the bad side of anarchy and it doesn't really work either.

– No... sigh... there is really no society working properly anywhere in the world.

Even if the republican dream flickers faintly in the blue beyond, the RS-ers stride onward and upward in their woolly socks, no, in their deck shoes.

There are general meetings every year, unsuccessful ones according to Per Edström who is regularly voted in as chairman "because I talk a lot and the others want to shut me up".

They arrange sailing races, like the silver cup race, an idea they took from KSSS.

A big thing in 1988 and 1989 was taking part in the international sailing regatta "Sailing for Peace", after the Soviet Union peace committee had freed up some money for them.

– That was a fine sail from Copenhagen to Lübeck and Rostock where we put on our play "Harlekin och Draken" (Harlequin and the Dragon) about a little man and a great big oppression. Fifty boats took part, several from the Baltic States and Russia. I think it did quite a lot of good.

– In November 1989 the wall fell...

What do Per Edström and his republicans think of the king?

– I feel sorry for him for having to be a symbol. But he copes as well as he can. Being a symbol is not easy. These things go in waves and monarchy is surfing along on the crest just now. But dark forces are gathering and new powers arising in the turbulence stirred up by the wave...and I mean the skin-heads and the racists.

– I heard the same unnatural nonsense in Östra Real in 1939–41 when not only the students but some of the teachers were swallowing the Nazi line.

Are you comparing monarchists with Nazis?

– They are not far apart. The same hierarchical system, the same process of selection, the same style of management and control. I will not go as far as to say they are the same. But you only have to get someone at the top who is a little extreme in one way or another and it does not work. It can be very tough at the top. But nobody gives that much thought at present.

– As long as we have this symbol of the king, society will not work properly. Officials and administrative types will always behave as if they have the king behind them.

Per Edström ends with an example of how the Palace played out the plot of "Harlekin och Draken" using their big power against the little individual – Per Edström himself.

Per Edström's life's work is his theatre-boat Arena, moored (with permission) on Skeppsholmen, opposite the Royal Palace in Stockholm.

With the republican flag flying from the top.

It was June 1976 and Sweden was gearing up for THE ROYAL WEDDING.

– Suddenly we were moved on. We were not allowed to stay flying our flag. The Palace had come up with quite an elegant solution: regrettably there had been a change in the route of the royal procession and the royal couple would need to board the "Vasa" launch just where "our" boat's pontoon happened to be.

Do you mean the Palace thought this up just to get rid of your republican flag?

– Of course! But I told them that we couldn't move the boat on that particular day because we would be away. Where are you going, asked the Palace. To the Soviet Union, I replied.

– That figures, was the Palace's reply!

The theatre-boat Arena got moved to the back side of Skeppsholmen. And Per Edström "celebrated" the Swedish royal wedding in Moscow.

Plenty of royalist ladies are to be found along the king's processional route.
PHOTO: SVEN STRÖM 1974

AS KING HE LOOKS STRAIGHT THROUGH US.

The king keeps separate, strictly separate, his two roles as king and as private person. In one role he behaves officially and according to protocol. In the other he is an easy-going and quick-witted fellow.

Just think what it is like being born to be king.

To be watched, talked about, looked after, discussed, analysed, joked about, written about, quoted, fussed over, photographed, admired, criticised, avoided, underrated, protected, cheered, stalked by the media, hugged, spied on, told off, played at by brass bands, respected, scheduled, waited on and guarded by military intelligence literally from cradle to grave.

It would not be easy. Nor is it.

– He would never have got the job if he had applied, wrote one journalist about the king. Many would certainly agree.

But perhaps more to the point, Carl Gustaf would probably never have thought of applying for the job of king given the choice.

As a boy he wanted to be a tractor driver. And now that he is grown up, he admits he would like to have been "something in farming or forestry".

But the fact is that this Carl Gustaf Folke Hubertus was born to be King of Sweden.

And in that role he draws a very sharp distinction between the scheduled official royal personage and the easy-going impulsive private person his friends know.

If someone tries to step over that line in either direction, the king becomes perplexed, pained and stiffens noticeably. He hates it when someone tries to force him to give up his king role by seeking to create some sort of informal "us-lads-together" atmosphere around him.

Once many years ago when the king visited Expressen in his official capacity to study the work of an evening newspaper over 24 hours, some hot-head hit upon the unscheduled idea of celebrating the king's presence with champagne in the editor-in-chief's office.

As long as the king was following the prearranged schedule in editing, typesetting and printing, everything was interesting and great and the king seemed pleased.

But when someone suddenly tried to cram twenty other people into the editor-in-chief Per Wrigstad's room with champagne corks popping at eleven o'clock in the morning, the king stiffened at once, hating to be put in this situation without any warning. The whole episode was a failure.

Another example: the king's state visit to Italy in 1991. When the royal entourage came to Venice, a gondola was brought up to the quay and the royal couple were invited to step down for a gondola tour.

It was intended as a PR-coup outside the programme. Beforehand the organisers had tried to induce the Palace to fit in a gondola trip, but the royal couple had said no. Snubbed once, the organisers effectively launched

The king photographed by an infrared camera during his visit to a technical fair in Budapest.
PHOTO: JOAKIM ROOS 1991

Out of the way for the king, here exercising with his regiment.

A thoughtful and frozen general warms his hands in a snowstorm. The king is the highest representative for navy, army and air force and is also admiral and double general.
PHOTO: PER LINDSTRÖM 1981

a sneak attack in the full glare of expectant Venetians, photographers and journalists. The king firmly refused, leading to sour looks in Venice and headlines and criticism back home.

– The king does not buy that sort of thing. Here he had the strength to resist the enormous pressure he was subjected to and which anybody else would have succumbed to. He knows that the timetable must be followed to the minute because further along the way there are other people and new delegations waiting, said somebody closely involved in the incident.

When the king is official he is KING.

The king's friends have discovered this whenever they have tried to step over the line between Carl Gustaf the king and Carl Gustaf the private person.

It will often be the case, for instance, that among a group of people waiting to greet the king officially and shake his hand, there are some personal friends or some officials he often meets and knows fairly well.

He never shows the slightest sign of recognition, not even "favouring" them with a special nod or a few words. And absolutely not with a kiss on the cheek or a hug!

– He looks straight through us, as if we did not exist. He even avoids greeting us, sighed one rather ruffled group of royal friends, while consoling themselves with the thought that "this was official".

Queen Silvia, Prince Bertil and Princess Lilian are quite different. In fact they are world champions at the art of the friendly greeting, asking about the children or exchanging a few words about when they last met.

This problem with the king's greetings is a story that runs and runs. And it is a continu-

ous source of irritation. Prince Bertil, advisers and all sorts of different Palace officials have over the years tried to teach the king the subtle art of greeting naturally in a relaxed manner. But to no avail.

A quote from Nenne Björnberg's book about the little prince:

– On occasions he refused to greet strangers, turning and looking the other way when someone spoke to him. If somebody came too close he became uneasy, wriggling away at on-ce if someone tried to assist him unnecessarily or take hold of him. He wanted to manage by himself and did not want to be nursed and pampered all the time. At the same time as a little boy he longed for affection, always wanting to be hugged and loving to cuddle up on somebody's lap.

Nowadays there is a chorus of complaints about the king's stiff and formal manner, his reserved and unnatural greetings, his failure to acknowledge people and his tendency to

A scout in the world. The king has been a scout from an early age and is nowadays chairman of the World Scout Foundation, an organisation which raises money for the scout movement. Here the king is addressing a scout meeting in Malmö.
PHOTO: ROLF OLSSON 1995

avoid eye contact when shaking hands. He lacks the ability to create an easy-going pleasant atmosphere when he greets people or enters a room. And he never seems to be able to say "thank you" in a nice way.

– He greets with his arm stretched out, as if he is trying to keep us away, was the conclusion one Conservative member of parliament came to.

– The king is not verbal but he has a distinctive body language, points out a close observer. He is somebody with strong emotions and opinions but instead of articulating them with words he uses gestures, facial expressions and body movements.

His whole upper body turns when he straightens his jacket. He is always looking at his watch. He hates making an entrance and at the Nobel ceremonies for instance, where he stands right

in the middle, he seems to almost fidget himself out of his seat, pulling at his clothes and looking in every possible direction as if he were looking for something.

He does not seem to enjoy the things he does officially and he often looks worried.

The little prince wriggling away from people and the king fidgeting out of his chair are indications perhaps of a long hard struggle against a deep-rooted shyness that has not gone unobserved.

The chorus of complaints has been given plenty of space for the simple reason that criticism of the king's manner of greeting people is in fact the only unanimously negative judgement about his official behaviour.

He is also said to make boring speeches that lack wit and substance, but this would seem to be more of a complaint against his speech writers than against the king himself.

Otherwise judgements of him as king are overwhelmingly positive. He fulfills his role as king conscientiously and ambitiously. His sense of duty is almost too extreme. He is punctual and well prepared.

The fact that he prepares well before his official engagements and is better informed than many people realise, is emphasised by everybody who has met the king in his working capacity.

He takes great care going through what is expected of him in the programme, he revises, checks facts, steps out distances and rehearses speeches, virtually knowing them by heart.

And the strange thing is that appreciation of the king crosses party lines with tory politicians if anything more critical than the social democrats and the socialists.

– I come from a very simple background, but the king has always treated me properly. There is not a whiff of superiority or arrogance about him.

– He is not a snob but a very democratic king, according to someone close to the social democratic government who has met the king on many occasions.

The king maintains a strictly neutral posture with regard to party politics and public statements (although sometimes his tongue slips as we know!).

He is regularly informed about the government's work and plans, by the prime minister and other ministers both at formal meetings and at the informatory council meetings.

But there are many who think the king ought to meet more informally with politically astute figures standing above party politics (Ulf Adelsohn, Odd Engström and Kjell-Olof Feldt for example). Such contacts would provide the king with a sense of the deeper political agendas beneath the day-to-day political events.

A final word from a well-known financier:

– The king is so damn Swedish!

The king and his family have the right to vote but by custom do not exercise it

– THE FIRST TIME THE KING LAUGHED BEFORE LUNCH.

His favourite expression is "bubbeli-bubb". And he likes dates with butter, a curious delicacy he picked up from Gustav V. He is particular about keeping his iron constitution and slim figure and jogs energetically around Drottningholm whenever he has an hour to spare. Previously he ran in Lill-Janskogen.

We have known he is good at sport ever since he first stood on skis as a three year old. Today Carl Gustaf skis downhill and cross-country and has two "Vasalopp" ski marathons under his belt. He also goes deep sea diving and swimming. But hunting is his favourite occupation and he can wax lyrical for hours about the beauty of animals and his experiences while out hunting.

He is quick and likes speed. He prefers to drive himself between his home at Drottningholm and his office at the Royal Palace in Stockholm. And on other trips he will often ask the chauffeur to sit in the back so that he can drive.

He is quick with his repartees, he has a well-developed sense of humour and enjoys irony and satirical exchanges. Where his responses seem slow in official situations, they are incisive and quick-witted when he engages in light-hearted conversation with his friends.

At a press conference in Brussels last autumn, the king won points for his quick-wittedness.

A journalist asked him how he felt about having his image removed from Swedish coins when the Euro replaces the krona.

– The king's picture on the krona has a strong symbolic value, ventured the journalist.

– What? The krona? Strong? retorted the king quick as a flash, diplomatically misunderstanding the question and using humour to lighten a situation at a time when the weakness of the krona was at the centre of a sensitive political debate in Sweden. The journalists languishing around the table burst out laughing, not out of politeness but because they appreciated the joke.

When the king travels to a place on an official visit he often takes the chance to check it out with a view to coming back later with his family.

Returning to Seville after the world fair for a private visit with the children, the royal couple spent several eventful and busy days shopping and sight-seeing before flying back to Arlanda early one evening.

All the royal family were worn out except father. After quickly repacking and changing clothes at Drottningholm, Carl Gustaf bundled the family and his aide into the motor boat Ancylus and set course for Solliden and a vacation.

While the family slept below, Carl Gustaf took the wheel and set off into the night, across Lake Mälaren, through Slussen and out into the Baltic, alone at the wheel. This is what he likes.

The king is interested in art and "objets d'art" and collects Swedish silver and glass. At the opening of an exhibition in Millesgården, Lidingö the king seems to be trying his best to imitate the sculptor Auguste Rodin's ideal of "the body elastic". *PHOTO: ANDERS KALLERSAND*

The motor yacht Ancylus (II) is the king's pride and joy. It has become something of a tradition for the boat to be moored up, cleaned out, maintained and ready to go on his birthday, May Day evening, for its annual maiden voyage with the family. Ancylus is the name of a type of shell.

Carl Gustaf also likes to drive his other sea-going vessel, an ex-Navy motor torpedo boat. When Sigtuna student anniversary time comes around, he packs all his old student friends into the boat and sails off for a trip on Lake Mälaren.

Carl Gustaf reads the daily newspapers Dagens Nyheter, Svenska Dagbladet, Expressen and Aftonbladet, watches television news and records those he does not have time for, which is most of them.

He does not read many books, mostly revision before forthcoming engagements. But there are books in his hand luggage when he travels by air. And in one interview he revealed that he had read "The Godfather" at least.

Despite coming from a culturally and artistically talented family, Carl Gustaf does not do anything artistic himself, apart from doodling in planning meetings and preparing food in the palace kitchens.

But over the years he has become more and more interested in art and nowadays likes to drop in at the National Museum at short notice for private viewings.

– He would never have done that 20 years ago, says one art curator while mentioning that the king saw the exhibition "Solen och Nordstjärnan" (Sun and the North Star) three times in Stockholm and once in Paris.

Carl Gustaf collects modern Swedish silver and Swedish glass from the 20s onwards, Vicke Lindstrand, Edvard Hald, Simon Gate, Eva Engström, Ulrika Hydman-Vallien and others, no doubt assisted by Louise Lyberg, the curator at Bukowski's and also a first lady of the court.

Some of the glass stays at home and some of it is used for gifts and presents.

Carl Gustaf may not be directly interested in art but he is fascinated by objets d'art, furniture and the contents of his royal palaces.

He reads the autumn and spring catalogues from the auction houses. Perhaps a sofa is up for sale or an ornamental clock that once long ago was in the royal collection. Is there a chance of buying it back and returning it to the collection?

Opera, concert hall and theatre directors miss the presence of Carl Gustaf and his family in their audiences. The royal boxes are seldom occupied. In Carl Gustaf's defence it might be said that he has only so much time and may well consider that his cultural needs are fulfilled by official events where music, choirs, theatre, appearances and performances abound.

Carl Gustaf likes to listen to music and has a large compact disc collection in his music corner. "Mostly modern" reads the brief list of contents.

Can he sing? He sings plenty of national anthems, but he can also switch to Swedish drinking songs. Some years ago at a semi-official crayfish party in Imatra, Finland, the king performed several amusing drinking songs while Queen Silvia sang some slightly more refined songs in Portuguese.

Squelch, squelch through the bog. The king needs boots to avoid getting stuck fast in the swampy ground during the annual royal invitation hunt in Hunneberg in Västergötland.
PHOTO: BERTIL PETTERSSON 1980

Any little prince would be shy when confronted with such a big boy bowing so low.
Quite a memory for the scout Åke Bergfelt who takes the seven year old prince's
hand and collects his silver trophy at the Mälarhöjden spring gathering.
IBL 1953

Earlier in 1973 the king, the foreign secretary Sven Andersson and the ambassador Sverker Åström were guests of the British royal family at Edinburgh Castle.

They are having a family evening at home in the castle apartments with the British royal family entertaining their guests. Princess Margaret is at the piano, the Queen Mother and Crown Prince Charles are dancing a gentle dance and everybody else is singing.

At the end the Swedish guests are asked to respond with a Swedish song.

A short and desperate conference: which one shall we go for?

Eventually the king, Andersson and Åström sing the only song all three of them know:

– "Sjungom studentens lyckliga dag" (Let's sing the praises of the student's happy day)...

It sounded absolutely terrible, but being well brought up, their audience applauded politely.

The king does not dance at official events because if he did he would have to dance with all the ladies in order of rank and somebody would always be upset and someone else offended.

But privately Carl Gustaf likes dancing as we have seen in innumerable glossy magazines ever since his years as the partying prince. Pictures of Carl Gustaf dancing with Pia Degermark were classics in their time the world over.

Carl Gustaf has resigned himself as king to having his diary regularly commandeered and his days filled up with programmes and schedules. From the moment he could stand on his little princely legs it has been this way.

This may explain why he keeps up such a hectic pace as a private person and is always busy doing something.

Friends state that he can fling himself down on a sofa and relax with a newspaper. But not for very long. Soon he must be up again, doing something, being busy and getting on.

A lady friend tells of a weekend at some palace out in the country. On Sunday morning the king and the other weekend guests came down for breakfast after partying through the night.

Out of consideration for his tired guests their host announced:

– We are having the day off, so relax, take it easy and do nothing.

But Carl Gustaf seemed completely mystified by the idea and soon became restless. No programme? Nothing to do? What are we going to do then?

Their host quickly reorganized for a fully-scheduled Sunday with a stroll, a boat trip, lunch and parlour games. The king liked that better.

– Carl Gustaf has lived with schedules since he was little. Removing the timetable is like taking off a corset; everything falls apart, explained the lady friend.

Cooking is one of his favourite pastimes. The weekend is sacred for Carl Gustaf for it is then he tries to spend as much time as possible with his family. The royal family are adept at mixing business with pleasure: saving money by giving the kitchen staff the weekend off while giving themselves unlimited access to the pots and pans.

They do not prepare anything remarkable. If the king and queen have eaten smoked salmon, steak and peach melba all week, then pasta with a simple sauce is quite a delicacy for Sunday dinner. Home cooked!

Carl Gustaf smokes, although he tries to give up, and cuts down his cigarette consumption with Nicorette nicotine chewing gum. He likes to drink wine, whisky and cognac where his iron constitution shows itself once more. Not many people have seen him really drunk.

Carl Gustaf is not at his best in the morning, a fact confirmed by nearly everyone. Those that know him assure us that he has now learned a few ways to cover this up.

– He has the same daily rhythm as Olof Palme. In a bad mood and hard to get going first thing, then thawing out as lunchtime approaches, before moving into top gear by the evening.

Once the royal couple dropped in for a private viewing at Moderna Museet. Suddenly the king pointed out the Julio Gonzales sculpture "Woman combing herself in front of the mirror", a prickly creation with hair straggling out in all directions.

– Just like Silvia in the morning, the king quipped making everybody laugh.

Afterwards one of the ladies of the palace commented:

– That's the first time I've seen the king laugh before lunch.

Carl Gustaf's friends are obviously very fond of him and fall over themselves to praise him. He is unbelievably loyal to his friends, considerate, a family man, socially talented, humorous, playful, inventive, and unfortunately sadly underrated by the media.

An example of his inventiveness. Last summer the royal couple attended an informal wedding of a friend out in the archipelago. The classic situation. Suddenly there was no ring for the marriage ceremony.

Take mine, says Carl Gustaf, taking off his ring with its royal crest.

– No, that won't do for their wedding ring, exclaims Silvia. So Carl Gustaf rushes into the house and moments later rushes out again with an ordinary brass curtain ring he has pulled down to save the situation.

He has a well-developed intuition and sound personal judgement, something which is very helpful when sorting out true friends from ingratiating flatterers seeking royal favours.

– He is no Einstein, but he has a way with people that makes him easy and pleasant to be around. I wish all journalists could get to hear him when he gets up and makes his amusing ad-lib speeches, says one highly talented female admirer who has known him for many years.

– Moreover he is well informed and knowledgeable – he has of course attended a fantastic "university", where he has had lectures on interesting subjects at least twice a day for twenty years.

– He takes in what he hears and is willing to share his knowledge in lively private conversations. Whether it is about the EU, currency union or whatever, he has something interesting to say the whole time.

However he never gives his personal opinion and never speaks ill of anyone, stiffening when anyone else makes personal criticisms.

Even if the "quality" of never criticising and putting people down can be attributed to his upbringing and self discipline, it is still remarkable – unique in fact – to be able to hold the neutral ground regardless.

– That is the compromise that Carl Gustaf has chosen. He knows that the slightest judgement, positive or negative, will be misused and cause trouble. "The king thinks this or that..." That could be devastating.

One friend of the king in the civil service criticises Carl Gustaf for moving in much too restrictive a circle of friends. He could draw many interesting people into his conversations and he should be able to surround himself with a circle of culture personalities, radical young civil servants and society debaters, meeting with them regularly to pick up a few fresh ideas.

King Carl Gustaf has the right to vote but by custom does not exercise it. He is not expected to express any political opinions, but his values are clearly bourgeois, and often extremely conservative, his friends tell us.

However he admired Olof Palme and enjoyed talking to Ingvar Carlsson.

When Olof Palme was murdered in 1986 the orders for the Royal Palace in Stockholm to fly the flag at half mast came from the king himself. This only normally happens when a member of the royal family dies.

Who is Carl Gustaf?

In the newspapers we read time and again that Carl Gustaf is a perfectly normal young fellow.

Now that he is 50 we should perhaps amend that and say instead:

Carl Gustaf is a quite ordinary man.

A royal team in keeping with the times. King Carl XVI Gustaf and Crown Princess Victoria, who from her 18th birthday may deputise for her father as the country's representative and head of state in his absence.
PHOTO: HANS T DAHLSKOG 1995

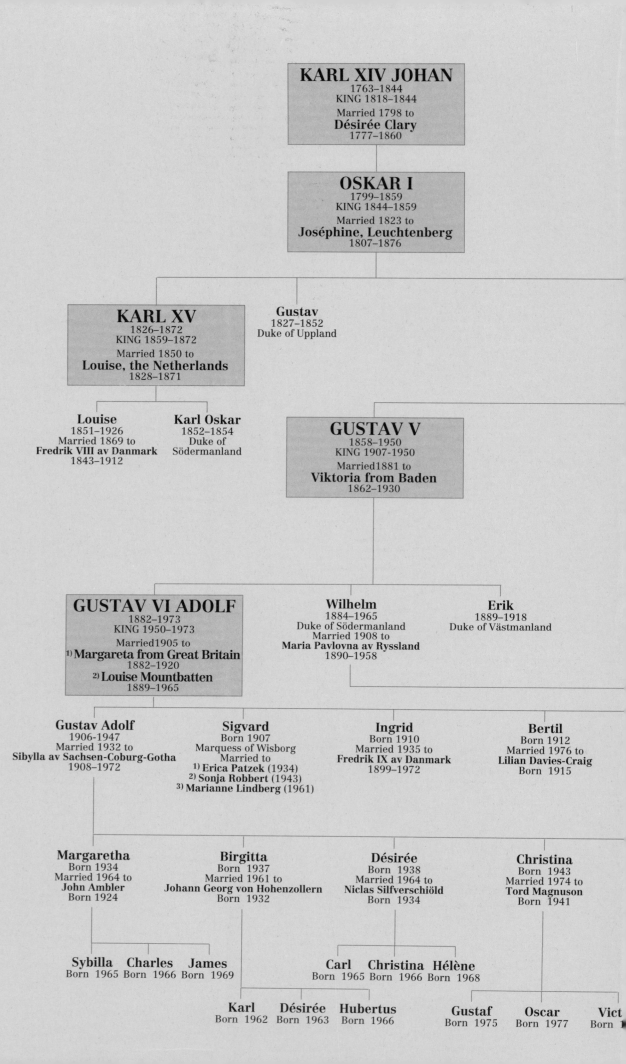

KARL XIV JOHAN
1763–1844
KING 1818–1844

Married 1798 to
Désirée Clary
1777–1860

OSKAR I
1799–1859
KING 1844–1859

Married 1823 to
Joséphine, Leuchtenberg
1807–1876

KARL XV
1826–1872
KING 1859–1872

Married 1850 to
Louise, the Netherlands
1828–1871

Gustav
1827–1852
Duke of Uppland

Louise
1851–1926
Married 1869 to
Fredrik VIII av Danmark
1843–1912

Karl Oskar
1852–1854
Duke of
Södermanland

GUSTAV V
1858–1950
KING 1907-1950

Married1881 to
Viktoria from Baden
1862–1930

GUSTAV VI ADOLF
1882–1973
KING 1950–1973

Married1905 to
[1] **Margareta from Great Britain**
1882–1920
[2] **Louise Mountbatten**
1889–1965

Wilhelm
1884–1965
Duke of Södermanland
Married 1908 to
Maria Pavlovna av Ryssland
1890–1958

Erik
1889–1918
Duke of Västmanland

Gustav Adolf
1906-1947
Married 1932 to
Sibylla av Sachsen-Coburg-Gotha
1908–1972

Sigvard
Born 1907
Marquess of Wisborg
Married to
[1] **Erica Patzek (1934)**
[2] **Sonja Robbert (1943)**
[3] **Marianne Lindberg (1961)**

Ingrid
Born 1910
Married 1935 to
Fredrik IX av Danmark
1899–1972

Bertil
Born 1912
Married 1976 to
Lilian Davies-Craig
Born 1915

Margaretha
Born 1934
Married 1964 to
John Ambler
Born 1924

Birgitta
Born 1937
Married 1961 to
Johann Georg von Hohenzollern
Born 1932

Désirée
Born 1938
Married 1964 to
Niclas Silfverschiöld
Born 1934

Christina
Born 1943
Married 1974 to
Tord Magnuson
Born 1941

Sybilla
Born 1965

Charles
Born 1966

James
Born 1969

Carl
Born 1965

Christina
Born 1966

Hélène
Born 1968

Karl
Born 1962

Désirée
Born 1963

Hubertus
Born 1966

Gustaf
Born 1975

Oscar
Born 1977

Vict
Born 1